LITTLE INNOCENTS

LITTLE INNOCENTS

CHILDHOOD REMINISCENCES

by

DAME ETHEL SMYTH
LORD BERNERS
HAROLD NICOLSON
DOROTHY WELLESLEY
LORD ALFRED DOUGLAS
EDMUND BLUNDEN
BARONESS RAVENSDALE
JAMES LAVER
SYLVIA PANKHURST
H. J. MASSINGHAM
ROSE MACAULAY
EDWARD SACKVILLE-WEST
ALICE, LADY LOWTHER
SONIA KEPPEL
ROBERT BYRON
PRINCESS ANTOINE BIBESCO
C. B. COCHRAN
LOUISA, COUNTESS OF ANTRIM
JOHN BETJEMAN
NINA HAMNETT
J. B. MORTON
EVELYN WAUGH
V. SACKVILLE-WEST
E. M. DELAFIELD
RAYMOND MORTIMER
LORD CLONMORE
BRIAN HOWARD
LADY LONGFORD
GERALD HEARD
J. C. SQUIRE

Preface by
ALAN PRYCE-JONES

Oxford   New York
OXFORD UNIVERSITY PRESS
1986

Oxford University Press, Walton Street, Oxford OX2 6DP

Oxford New York Toronto
Delhi Bombay Calcutta Madras Karachi
Kuala Lumpur Singapore Hong Kong Tokyo
Nairobi Dar es Salaam Cape Town
Melbourne Auckland

and associated companies in
Beirut Berlin Ibadan Nicosia

Oxford is a trade mark of Oxford University Press

First published 1932 by Cobden-Sanderson Ltd.
First issued as an Oxford University Press paperback 1986

British Library Cataloguing in Publication Data

Little innocents : childhood reminiscences.
1. Great Britain—Social life and customs—
19th century 2. Great Britain—Social life
and customs—20th century
I. Smyth, Ethell
941.082   DA533
ISBN 0-19-281943-7

Library of Congress Cataloging in Publication Data
Little innocents.
1. Children—Great Britain—Biography.
2. Great Britain—Biography. I. Smyth, Ethel, 1858–1944.
II. Pryce-Jones, Alan, 1908–
CT783.L57 1986   941'.009'92 [B]   86-2423
ISBN 0-19-281943-7 (pbk.)

Printed in Great Britain by
The Guernsey Press Co. Ltd.
Guernsey, Channel Islands

CONTENTS

v

Preface

AN EDITOR'S FUNCTION, WHICH IS NEITHER MORE IMPORTANT
nor more exhilarating to watch than that of the chairman at
a banquet, demands the same apology and the same slightly
nervous expedition. He is supposed to be conscious of the
reader hard at his heels, leaping his pages at a bound, in
search of the real matter beyond them; he is told to his face,
if only by the publisher, that he is a bore. "And mind,"
says that personage, "on no account more than two pages."
The apposite stories, the delicate points of wit, the genuine
beauty of his own memories, are thus rudely checked, and
the silver tongue which might so exaltedly have spoken is
silenced, if such a thing be possible, by a common blue
pencil.

So I will only allow myself to recall *The Annual* and *The
Keepsake* of former years, and to prophesy that the present
volume will not be found altogether unworthy of them.
Some of the distinguished faces which appeared in those
earlier volumes will be found between these covers, chubbier
perhaps, pinker even, but endowed already with a something,

a glow of promise, an assurance that the hoop bowled further, the ball bounced higher, in *their* hand; that the sweet sank with more conscious sweetness into *their* luxurious insides. And apart from these, there are new faces—Mr. Cochran to marshal them all in front of the curtain (but a tiny Mr. Cochran and rather an unhappy one); Lord Alfred Douglas, who might reduce the others to tears by beating them in their races were it not that he is older than they are, and therefore Miss Keppel's nanny will tell him it is unfair; Lady Antrim, whose Victorian childhood has, I am afraid, not quite the propriety which we are taught to expect of her contemporaries; Mr. Evelyn Waugh, interposing a stern little figure between the other children and the racecourse.

The order of the book has been decided in the same manner as the order of the *Keepsake*—namely by drawing the names of the contributors from a publisher's hat. And, lastly, the title. Frankly, we have called the book *Little Innocents* because of the extraordinary sophistication of these children. It is not my place to censor, scarcely even to rebuke, but I cannot but say that it seems to be just as well that most of the children never met Elisha on their walks; and of some, that it is a singular sign of the mercy of Providence that their nurseries were not laid waste by fire and the sword.

"Only . . ."

THE OTHER DAY AT WOKING, NEAR WHICH THRIVING suburb of London I have the honour to dwell, someone fell out of a bus opposite my cottage. Hearing about it on my return from London, I remarked to the bus-driver: "I hope it wasn't Mary" (my servant); whereupon he replied: "Oh no; it was only Mrs. H."

Now Mrs. H., though fattish and far from agile, is not a reveller, so there was nothing of the foregone conclusion about her landing in the road on all fours, nor did the word "only" betoken indifference on the part of the kindly busman to a passenger's abrased knees; it was merely that in his desire to allay my personal anxiety it popped out unawares.

While I was still smiling secretly—who could help it?—at the turn of this phrase, one of those mysteries of memory happened to which we never get accustomed. Suddenly stood out in my brain, as on a screen at a film, an exactly similar phrase of which I had never thought since the day on which it was spoken; this, although the occasion which called it forth, a boating incident of my childhood, found passing mention in my autobiography "Impressions that Remained"!

At the time those four words were uttered they made no sort of impression on me, one way or the other. Of that I am perfectly certain. Why then should they suddenly flare up out of the past in a Woking bus in the year 1932? It's really very odd. But then, nearly everything is very odd. Anyhow here's the story.

Eastern philosophers have remarked, not without a touch of contempt, that we of the West set an exaggerated value on life. If this impeachment be deserved—and it probably is —all the prouder am I to reflect that my father, an instinctive opponent of the "Safety-first" School, never had cause to complain of lack of readiness on the part of his progeny to take risks.

On the other hand, as regards their pets the imagination of his children was vivid, tender-fibred, and hysterical. I know that one of my everlasting nocturnal terrors, followed by a barefoot excursion to the nursery, was that the canary's water having been forgotten he was now lying stiff and stark, toes upwards, on the floor of his cage. Another was round about the watery death, as described by a farm-bred nursery maid, of her father's prize heifer, stream and animal figuring of course in the nightmare as a pet lamb and the duck pond. And another concerned the cat, for we had yet to learn that the notes put forth so oft in the stilly night by cats are identical, whether it be love or a rabbit-trap that has them in its fangs. I was going to add, that when one of the horse accidents happened for which "The Smyth Family Robinson" became notorious (as could only be expected, given my father's fancy for bargains in young and untrained horse-flesh) the first question put, even by him, was always: "Is the horse damaged?" But on reflection I think this solicitude was referable to the never very flourishing state of our finances, combined with a conviction that his offspring had a knack of falling on their feet.

Meanwhile the passion of us children for every sort of pet-donkeys, ponies, lambs, young pigs (I once owned a young pig called Fairylight), lop-eared rabbits, cats, and above all dogs, was a by-word in the village. For Frimley began life as a village, hard as it is to believe it now. In fact, one day, shortly after some particularly unpleasant murder had taken place, I remember my father, who admired Wordsworth and Gray, referring to Frimley as "this peaceful hamlet."

Chiefest, surely, in the long list of all our pets, was a certain jet black spaniel, Kitty by name, who, like other English "favourites," specially in the Chronicles of Art, had achieved this pre-eminent position by the simple process of living to a great age. At the time of which I am speaking Kitty was old, asthmatic, rheumatic, exceedingly stout, and said to be suffering from a heart complaint, which, if we persisted in throwing sticks into the water for her to retrieve, might at any moment end in tragedy. Consequently, in our many boating expeditions on the Basingstoke Canal, which skirted our home, Kitty was carefully conducted in and out of the boat and given to understand that the only things expected of her were to wait her turn and sit quiet once she was in. This was incidentally a good plan for all concerned, the mud in that canal, specially in our section where it runs through peat, being of a blackness that must be seen to be believed.

One day, the occasion being the tenth birthday of my sister Nina, the fleet consisted of a four-oared boat—leaky, but fast and reliable—and a canoe propelled by Nina, on the prow of which, as special birthday treat, Kitty was installed. It was by no means the first time she had thus travelled; and being extremely broad in the beam, with a natural instinct of self-preservation reinforced (as always happens) by years, there was no cause for anxiety.

3

The boat was leading the procession, followed deviously and at some distance by the canoe, when, arrived at the end of a long straight stretch of water, it became manifest that our follower was out of sight. Greatly agitated, though solely on Kitty's account, two of us leaped ashore and began tearing back along the towing path, holding up on the way an exceedingly idiotic little boy whom we began to interrogate—no doubt in an excited and incoherent manner. Had he seen a canoe and a little girl and a dog, a *black* dog? (He had.) What was the dog doing? (Trying to get out of the water.) *Had* she got out? . . . But the child becoming more and more vague under cross-examination and time being of value, we fled on, shouting "Kitty! Kitty!" and presently encountered a slightly inebriated patriach of the village—a sort of family friend who was in the custom of lending amateur aid to Mr. Lidbetter, the Vet, at critical moments in farmyard life. "Have you seen Kitty?" we bawled. "I seed an overturned boat," he replied. "But Kitty . . . *Kitty* . . . is she safe?" we asked in agony. "I dunno," he said. "I 'spect so, but she was that waterlogged, strugglin' in the weeds and mud, that I did think she'd never get out." "But *did* she get out?" "Oh yes," he remarked ruminatingly. "She got *out* all right . . . lyin' on the towing path she is, a puffin' and a blowin' like anythink" . . .

One of us burst into tears: "You know what Lidbetter said" (she sobbed to the other) "that she'd die if we let her swim a yard!" A look of bewilderment came over the face of the patriarch. "*Lidbetter* . . ?" he said. "You're talkin' about the *dog*, are you? Bless your hearts, there ain't nothin' to cry about; *she's* all right . . . shakin' 'erself she was and rollin' in 'orse-muck when I went by! . .No . . no," he quavered, unsteadily pursuing his way, "what I see crawlin' out of the water . . . black as pitch she was to be sure . . . *was only Miss Nina*."

Neighbours

ABOUT FOUR MILES FROM MY HOME THERE LIVED AN elderly lady, Mrs. Lafontaine, and her companion, Miss Goby. They were fond of children, and I was often invited to go over and spend the afternoon with them. At that time I had never been abroad, and these two ladies represented to my eager imagination the glamour of foreign travel. Each year they went for a sketching tour on the Continent and brought back portfolios filled with water-colours of France, Switzerland or Italy, executed with a skilful combination of accuracy and romance.

Mrs. Lafontaine and her companion belonged to a certain type of Englishwoman that is still happily to be met with on the Continent. They both had the slightly prominent teeth of the traditional "fille d'Albion" of French caricature. Their high fringes were surmounted by hats perched at an angle that made them look as though they were about to loop the loop. Their movements were brisk and decided; their voices loud and authoritative. One could visualise them moving through foreign crowds, oblivious of mockery,

5

wholly concentrated on the enjoyment of "being abroad."

For them the Continent had still the flavour of the eighteenth century Grand Tour, with perhaps a touch of Mark Twain's *Innocents Abroad*. For them Germany was still the Germany of Goethe; France, the France of the first English settlers on the Riviera; and Switzerland, devoid of sanatoriums and winter sports, the Switzerland of edelweiss, William Tell and the Merry Swiss Boy.

Mrs. Lafontaine's house was called "Rose Hill." It stood as its name implied, on a hill, and its trellised porches were festooned with roses. The interior of the house had a very pronounced Italian atmosphere. The rooms were filled with mosaic cabinets, striped fabrics from Sorrento, inlaid wooden boxes, painted Venetian furniture, goblets and chandeliers of Murano glass. In the hall there was a stone fire-place transported from Bologna. The food also was in the Italian style, and one had risotto, macaroni and, a delicacy I particularly delighted in, raisins folded in vine leaves and tasting of wedding cake.

In the summer the two ladies would sometimes take me with them to picnic by the river side. We would drive down through the park in a pony-chaise followed by a footman in another cart carrying the tea things and sketching appliances. The sketches they made of the neighbourhood had the same romantic qualities as those painted abroad. I was very happy in their company, and I looked up to "Rose Hill" as to a little Valhalla of art and culture.

As I grew older I began to discover that most of my companions considered Mrs. Lafontaine and Miss Goby to be figures of fun. I grew to be ashamed of my friendship with the two ladies of "Rose Hill." As I passed from childhood to adolescence I lost my independence of spirit. My judgment became more and more influenced by public opinion. I began to refuse their invitations. After I went to school I saw very little of my former friends and the memory of all

6

the happy afternoons spent at "Rose Hill," the picnics by
the river, the excitement of examining a new batch of
Continental landscapes, the delicious Italian food—all this
was for the time obliterated by a growing sense of the
ridiculous which, in its early stages, made me self-conscious
and fearful of being associated with things and people
generally considered to be absurd. I was at that time very
far from that enlightened stage in which it is possible to
combine mockery with affection and to disentangle the
sublime from the ridiculous. Not that there was anything
very sublime about the two ladies of "Rose Hill," but there
was much that was lovable and, from my own particular
point of view, helpful and stimulating.

Mrs. Lafontaine and Miss Goby are dead. But the re-
membrance of the pleasant hours spent in their company, of
all that they meant for me at a certain period of my childhood, of their kindness and their absurdity, has left in my
mind a trail of melancholy and remorse.

There was another neighbour who stood out from the background of more conventional county folk. This was Mr.
Vivian Pratt.

Distantly connected with a ducal family, he enjoyed more
consideration than he might otherwise have done. Mr.
Vivian Pratt was considered eccentric but amusing. Country
people in the 'nineties were apt to be a little naïve with
regard to certain aspects of life. It was said of Mr. Pratt that
he was rather odd and inclined to effeminacy, but that was
all. He had a mincingly ingratiating voice, and he moved
with an undulating gait. In walking through a room he
looked as though he were avoiding imaginary tables and
chairs and he would describe elaborate circles with the
middle portion of his body. His clothes had a fashion-plate
neatness, and seemed inappropriate to the country. When
he appeared on horseback nobody could present a more

7

dapper appearance of horsiness, but his get-up, like that of Miss Lucy Glitters, looked as though it could hardly have weathered a rain-storm.

His manners were almost excessive in their courtliness, and he embarrassed my mother by addressing her as "Dear Lady." His conversation consisted chiefly of anecdotes relating to London society or the theatrical world. I gathered that my father did not care very much for Mr. Pratt. His behaviour when Mr. Pratt was present and his comments after he had left seemed to suggest that he understood him better than my mother and the rest of the countryside appeared to do. I remember on one occasion when Mr. Pratt said: "I often think that the best things in life are behind us," my father broke out into a cynical guffaw, which seemed to me to be quite unwarranted by the sentimental character of the remark.

I too did not care very much for Mr. Pratt. Chiefly, I think, because he did not seem to be the least interested in children, and when he came to call he appeared to regard me rather as a nuisance than anything else. However, one day, when I rode over to his house with a note from my mother, he made himself unexpectedly agreeable. He showed me his collection of jade and his orchid houses. When I left he thrust an orchid into my hand. My mother, upon my showing it to her on my return, displayed an unaccountable irritation. She said it was a ridiculous thing to have given a child. I imagine that the exotic nature of the gift must have aroused for the first time a dim suspicion in her unsophisticated mind.

After this visit I thought a little better of Mr. Pratt. I was accompanied at the time by a rather good-looking groom and I remember telling myself that, after all, he must be a nice man to be so unusually amiable and condescending to servants.

Many years later I came across Mr. Pratt again in Paris

just after the war. He had been working in connection with the Red Cross. The patina of time seemed to have improved him. There were still unmistakable indications for the pathologist, but his voice had grown less mincing; his gait less undulating. The impression I had may have been due to the fact that he was wearing a uniform which, as the term implies, has a tendency to minimise irregular characteristics, or, more probably, because I had grown accustomed to a type which, in the intervening years, had come into its own.

"Pure in Heart"

'NO!' SAID MISS WELLAN. 'NO, DEAR, ONLY THE PURE IN HEART.'

I was worried by this, scenting Gregory powder; and yet anxious that I, also, might receive the call.

Miss Wellan's own call had occurred one November morning in the year 1856. She had just, for the fourth time, told me all about it. I was sitting at the piano stool, and in front of me was spread that reiterant tune, "Der Lustige Bauer." My father, having himself a liking for Rossini, imagined that I was musical. It has taken me some thirty-five years to probe the full depths of that misapprehension. But at the time (in the year that is 1896) I believed that my father, as usual, was right. I was nine years old. I flung myself into the Lustige Bauer with that abandon which I have since observed in the attitude of Rubinstein, Lord Berners, Mr. Sackville-West, Sir Thomas Beecham, and others of my musical friends. Without a word of protest I had allowed Miss Wellan—with her unfortunately protrudent tooth—to be added to Miss Plimsoll, who did not teach the pianoforte and was at any rate, at that period, in a mood of declination.

And it was thus Miss Wellan who ("*tum, tum*—one, two, *tam, tam*—one, two; no dear, let's begin again") ministered to my square uncertain fingers.

Miss Wellan, by profession, was what, at the close of the nineteenth century, was called "A Lady Missionary." She had been a lady missionary for some forty years. It was during my third lesson in the intricate art of playing the Lustige Bauer that she told me how her vocation had come to her. And as, with succeeding lessons, my interest in the Lustige Bauer declined, my interest in Miss Wellan's vocation increased. I found that with slight inducement she would abandon that tiresome metronomic scansion of the Lustige Bauer, and would revert, with a sudden flattening of the voice, with a half closure of a freckled eyelid, to that Sunday morning of 1856, when she received her call.

The very moment at which God had informed her that among the many eligible gentlewomen of Tunbridge Wells, she—Mabel Wellan—had been selected to convert the North African heathen remained for her a constant and vivid point of reminiscence. I enjoyed the story, not merely as a welcome interlude in that half-hour of already distasteful music, but as an illustration of the very intimate, if somewhat haphazard, relations which it was possible for very gifted people to establish with the Deity.

"I remember all too well," Miss Wellan would begin. "It was a Sunday morning in November. I had been learning the Collect, and realised suddenly that I should have to hurry if I were not to be late for church. I ran up the stairs to my little attic bedroom. It was as if a voice, rather like my dear Uncle's voice, spoke from behind me. 'Mabel,' said the voice, 'be prepared.' My heart beat wildly"—Miss Wellan would pause at this stage allowing her single tooth to find its accustomed resting-place upon her lower lip—"*wildly*. I knew at once. I *knew*. Yes, dear, I *knew* from that moment that I had been chosen to guide those who walk in darkness."

The choice, I have since reflected, was a poor one. Miss Wellan had come to Morocco determined to convert the heathen; she had ended by giving prizes to those of the donkey boys who refrained from sticking aloe thorns into the hindquarters of their beasts. She was known locally as "the donkey missionary." Yet, perhaps, she responded more fully to that vocation than to her timid, her very uncertain, attempts to wean her housemaid from the tenets of Islam.

"That," Miss Wellan would conclude, flinging her little sparrow head backwards with the gesture of Napoleon at Erfurt, "that was how I received the call."

"And do you think, Miss Wellan," I asked her at the fourth narration, "do you think that God would come to me also?"

Miss Wellan was clearly embarrassed by this question. After all, she had been engaged to teach me the Lustige Bauer and not in the least for the purpose of preparing me for any other sort of call.

"No," she answered, "only the pure in heart can receive this message."

I have since reflected that this evasion on the part of Miss Wellan savoured of spiritual arrogance. Yet at the time I was impressed. I was not certain what was actually meant by that adjective "pure" or even by that substantive "heart." The former, owing mainly to the flat voice employed by Miss Wellan in stressing it, was obviously spiritual. The latter, however, was to my certain knowledge, internal. And, disliking internal complaints, I decided to keep this purity of heart to myself. True it is that, at tea that afternoon, I asked Lady Harris, the widow of an official, whether she was pure of heart. I had to repeat the question, Lady Harris being infirm and scant of hearing. It was not a successful question. She looked at me a trifle startled and

12

answered: "Well, I hope so, dearie." I was glad then that I had not asked my father, but only Lady Harris.

It is difficult for me to recapture the exact stages of my subsequent problem. I know only that my energies of thought thereafter concentrated, not so much upon receiving the call (although I have a distinct memory of trying to learn Collects, running upstairs and thinking hard about my uncle), as upon the business about pure of heart. I would repeat the words to myself secretly until they ceased to have any but a narcotic meaning. And to this day the phrase awakes in me a dim mysticism, through which glimmer the picture of Lady Harris looking at me embarrassed over her steel glasses, of myself murmuring the words among the arum lilies, of Miss Wellan, with her brown little tooth above her lower lip, of Miss Wellan recalling in the glow of her little pippin face that moment of annunciation in her attic bedroom of 1856.

"No, dear, only the pure in heart . . ."

Perhaps she was right. Yet it would have been another mistake, now I come to think of it, had I been really asked to guide those who, in Morocco, walk in darkness.

Infancy

I STARE INTO A FULL-LENGTH MIRROR FACING ANOTHER mirror. The reflections—rows of halma men—at last dwindle and merge. I dodge them, trying to get a better view of the last one. I give it up. The first figure blots out the last figure in the remote vista of glass.

One tries to remember more, still more. There were events in early childhood, journeys, deaths of relations, and so on, that have left no seal upon the wax. Insignificant incidents are sealed clear-cut on the memory. As I grow older I remember more. Sometimes in the state between waking and sleeping I remember something that happened years ago. I wake with a start. A shaft of light has stabbed the room, lighted up a medallion in the darkness. There it is, there it has always been, but now clear, sharp in detail. "I had forgotten that," I say. "Yes, of course, myself, trying to climb up the brass bars of a cot, brass bars with green smudges, when the nurse had left me to sleep; and I climbed out at last and crawled, as I couldn't walk far, and sat on the top stair to listen for her return from supper. Very remote. I remember the pattern of the carpet; it was striped like Joseph's coat in many colours. A dog that died before I was three, a Skye dog I had forgotten called Topsy; and, yes, she had a sore on her back; I didn't like the sore; and how could she walk without legs, and see without eyes? Trees outside the nursery window, trees soughing, lit (as I know now) like trees on a stage."

I always wish that people would tell me about their earliest memories. I have noticed that if one questions them they almost invariably lose interest in the conversation. Now this is either because they do not remember, or because they do not wish to remember. And perhaps this is so because all children, certainly all small children, are always a little anxious. This cannot be otherwise. Fear of punishment, fear of scolding, even of a snub. And then the horror of the food which one had to eat when one didn't like it, and the misery of the daily walk. A child's waking moment might well be darkened by the prospect of that inevitable walk. It is not natural for children to walk. As well take a marmoset for a walk. This at least might provide better entertainment for the nurse. The lagging of that child, the shouting of that nurse!

Perhaps therefore the normal adult subconsciously forgets infancy because he was always a little anxious or afraid. If however his memory is jogged at a suitable moment, if, for instance, one asks: "When you were a child did you think that telegrams flew down the wires, orange envelopes revolving rapidly like wheels between two persons?" he will probably give an imperceptible start and answer: "Yes, I did." His memory has been jogged, that is all. If one develops the telegraph-poles theme (it absorbed my infant imagination) and says: "Did you like the whining sound in a wind, and stand by the poles to listen while your nurse had walked on, and think—That whining noise is all the messages in the world going along?" the adult, especially the

15

middle-aged adult, if this question does not make him shy, will probably answer: "Yes." If you push on a little further and ask: "Did you think the white jars on the telegraph poles were filled with different kinds of jam, yet wonder why it was necessary to have jam-pots to send telegrams?"—if you ask this, you may fail to get a satisfactory answer, for it is not every child that believes in the jam-pot theory.

By questions and answers such as these one may fairly establish that the minds of all infants work on much the same lines. Later on people have forgotten or have not forgotten, that is all.

There were many theories of the same kind, brutally logical. "Yesterday it rained in London; not here. Why can't I find the edge of the rain? If it rains on one side of the house so that I may not go out, why don't people go to see if it's raining on the other side of the house too? Why don't cows mind walking about and lying down on their food? We should hate to lie down on fields of marmalade, and walk about in meadows of buttered eggs." And again, "As all living creatures in Siam are twins and stuck together, how do they manage the natural but so interesting functions of daily life?" Again, the South Pole was hot. Ladies with long skirts were completely solid from top to toe, but when they sat down and the fundament came into play, it was obvious that they were also jointed, like dolls. Scarecrows were dead men set to divert the appetites of crows, and hat-pins went bang through ladies' heads. Why didn't they mind?

I find that memories from time to time return, slight, difficult to seize. I see infancy as a pale luminous picture, like the later sketches of Turner. I say infancy rather than childhood, because these experiences occurred before I was four years old—years extraordinarily exciting, life overflowing, all colour, above everything enchanted. A rainbow set down on a ploughed field far away. "Can I get there in time?" There were many such things outdoors; few in the house. Indoors, the fire, colour of wine, sound of music; but, beyond such lovely things, there was no enchantment within walls. Outdoors it was always summer, warm luminous summer. This was because of the leaves, leaves soughing, leaves lit, or heavy, silent before a storm, leaves pattering under thunder drops, oak leaves with intricate edges, lime leaves honeycombed by caterpillars, mulberry leaves rough like the chins of old men who kissed one, young chestnut leaves like hanging fingers, young beech leaves lovely beyond belief. I have never read a line from any book by Freud or Jung; but what is this?—

> "Hush-a-bye, baby, on the tree-top,
> When the wind blows the cradle will rock,
> When the bough breaks the cradle will fall,
> Down will come cradle, baby and all."

A cradle in a tree-top? Who ever put one there? Has no one ever been interested by this verse? Was it written by someone whose memory acted for a moment by instinct, who remembered a platform of boughs in a tree-top, the peace of the swinging, the terror of the fall? Or was it written by a child?

Somewhere or other I must have read or heard the fifteenth century lines:

> "All under the leaves and the leaves of life
>   I met with Virgins seven,
>   And one of them was Mary mild
>   Our Lord's mother of heaven."

I remember a child alone in a wood anxiously lifting leaf after leaf of a chestnut tree in the hope of finding, firstly, the Virgins Seven (whatever that might be); and, secondly, with luck, the Virgin Mary herself, complete with the Holy Child.

Now foreigners, especially the French, tell us that we have never acquired the adult mind. I think they are right. But I, being English, have never quite lost an early impression of life as set down in these lines:—

CHEMISTS' JARS

At night they glow; Arabian gems,
    Great on the little shelves.
The emerald high-road, golden Thames,
    They hold within themselves.

Banked up by Eno's Fruit Salt,
Inhaling-tubes and trusses,
These bottles show me walking by
With dolls or blunderbusses.
Oh! upside down in scarlet streets
Old ladies catch the buses;
Oh! tiny policemen wave and roar,
Oh! upside down for ever more
The population fusses
About the drains and all the things
The Alderman discusses.

Winning the Steeplechase at Winchester

THE HAPPIEST DAY OF MY LIFE WAS THE DAY I WON THE school steeplechase, two and a-half miles across country, at Winchester. Or was it only the happiest day of my child-hood? In any case it was wonderful, and when I think of it I can still bring back some of the rapture. The steeplechase was run over natural ground, including at least one ploughed field, and a stiffish uphill slope of about half a mile. My winning had, for me, all the pleasurable thrill of backing a winner at long odds (which still occasionally happens even in "this sad late day"), immeasurably intensified by the fact that I did it all myself, without the assistance of a horse and a jockey and a race-course, let alone a bookmaker. If there had been any betting on the event I would certainly have been at 100 to 1. Nobody except myself had the slightest idea that I had a chance. My particular friend at the moment was a boy with bright red hair, who was known in our house as "Young Bar" (his brother being "Old Bar"), and to his "pregnant and vouchsafèd ear" I revealed the secret that I was going to win. He was an amiable and kindly youth, and he endeavoured without success to conceal his incredulity.

The race was a handicap, or really it would better be described in racing language as "weight for age, with penalties and allowances." That is to say, you were handicapped according to your age, but if you had won the race before, or figured in the first three, or had any other "public form," you were additionally docked of start.

As I had never run in the race before and was sixteen and a-half, I had, so far as I can remember, 120 yards start. There was a very large field, certainly not less than a hundred runners. The boy who was "limit" had about 400 yards start. I told Young Bar that I was going to win, and Young Bar said: "Good for you, Bosie," but I felt that he thought I was raving. My confidence was based entirely on private runs I had been taking. I knew I could run for miles and that the further I went the better I felt. I was not very fast. At anything less than a mile I was no good, but I was what the sporting writers used to call "one who will be running on when others are stopping," and I could pull out a good final spurt even when I was in distress.

As I stood waiting for the pistol my heart was in my boots. Young Bar, who was not running in the race, stood close at hand and surveyed me with a sympathetic grin.

The pistol went off, and I started to run in my zephyr and bare legs, but not in spiked running shoes, if I remember right. Before I had gone 200 yards I had dropped back a lot, and, after going threequarters of a mile, I had been passed by scratch and many more who had started behind me. I began to feel that I had no earthly chance and to wish I were dead—or at least that I had never started. I could not quicken my pace without completely knocking myself out; and I seemed to be running very slowly. As we went up the long hill we went slower and slower, but already those in front were "coming back to me." When I got to the top of the hill with about a mile and a bit to go I had got my second wind, and began to run easily, increasing my pace. In the next quarter of a mile I passed at least fifty runners, many of whom had stopped dead and were walking. I felt perfectly well, except that the excitement made me almost sick.

I ran on blindly, beginning at last to feel that I was getting to the end of my tether, and that in any case I could not possibly go any faster, when suddenly a mob of boys out of my own house—among them the two Weatherbys and "Sal" Phipps—appeared from nowhere, yelling encouragement: "Go it, Alf!" (I was indifferently "Alf" or "Bosie" in my house.) "There are only three in front of you!"

By this time the ground was sloping down, and I could see the three in front of me. I bore down on them and passed the nearest two, but the one in front—"Young Morsehead," who won the race in the following year—was still a hundred yards in front of me. Gradually I wore him down and drew up to him. For fifty yards we ran neck and neck. Then he gave a grunt and fell back beaten, and I went on to win with great ease by several hundred yards, though I nearly came to grief at the last "fence" but one. There was no question of jumping these natural fences or obstacles. It was a case mostly of scrambling or climbing. As I breasted the tape and fell over on to the grass I thought I was dreaming, for my young brother Sholto was bending over me and saying: "Bravo, Bosie; splendid!" I had not the slightest idea he was there. He was at a private school in Winchester, and I had no knowledge that the boys of his school had been brought out by a master to watch the finish of the Steeplechase.

I lay panting in complete ecstasy for five minutes, and then went back to my house surrounded by an enthusiastic escort.

The most unhappy day of my childhood (if not of my life) was exactly a year later when the Steeplechase was run again, and I was in bed in the "sick-room" with a bad sore throat. I was perfectly certain, I thought, to win again, this time from scratch. I was so fit that I used to run ten or twelve miles, and come back by way of St. Cross, jumping all the five-barred gates in my stride—I think there were six of them. I feel sure I would have won it again and won it easily, but three days before the race I developed a sore throat and a temperature. All sorts of appalling misfortunes and miseries have come to me since; but I do not think I have ever suffered more in my mind than I did then.

I hope all this does not sound too egoistical, but I must just add that when I won, dear old Fort (one of the masters, or "dons," as they are called at Winchester) was so impressed by the fast time I put up that he got up at five o'clock next morning, and, to use his own words, "ran a chain over the course." He thought the time was too good to be true; but it was not. I do not know if there is any record kept of the times at Winchester. If there is one, I should very much like to know if my time was later equalled or beaten.

Bells on the Breeze

A KINDLY TRAMP, WITH FLAMING BEARD, MET ME AT THE far end of the lane as I was coming through the kissing-gate, carrying a yellow flag-flower and a white water-lily (already strangely disenchanted). I was also eating a green apple, my first of the season. He spoke: "Don't eat that, Jack; it'll give you the Guts'-Ache." My ears tingled; I blushed—my only answer; what could I say? "Guts"; what language! It was as though the blue sky had turned rusty. In one monosyllable, the scaly depravity of the human spirit seemed revealed to me. I hurried from the scene of slaughtered innocence; and the queer thing is that when I pass that scene this afternoon on the way to our village cricket, my mind will feel a trifle uneasy, Edenless. . . .

But that first cricket match went off without a shadow. I was in the village choir from the earliest possible age, not so much for musical as for moral and cautionary reasons; and every year the boys of the great houses of our parish, released from their preparatory schools, challenged the choir to a cricket match. I found myself, by one means or another, included in the choir team, and at last my turn (No. 11) came to go in. At the other end was "Froggy," the youth who had been beating the ball in all directions. I was received with compassion; the bowlers treated me to lobs. This went on until they were tired of it, and they began "hurling them down." I survived that just long enough for Froggy to reach his century; I had nineteen, and then observed that my stumps were at angles. How joyfully I walked beside Froggy towards the pavilion, in that golden sunshine, tasting honour and glory! Now I come to think of it, the applause would have been for the youth whose whizzing hits had gathered a hundred runs; but I did not at the time go into the niceties of the case—we were a triumphant pair of batsmen.

Practice for such crises as that had been carried on with a rag ball, at making which Mrs. C., of Church Cottages, was wonderfully quick and expert; but still, we pined for something superior, something which would fly farther. Butler's shop sold fine rubber balls, price twopence; and one day the curate's wife, a lady of a primrose-like complexion, whose smile was to me angelical, gave me some notes to deliver here and there and twopence for doing so. Scrambling through my round, I darted to Church Cottages and showed A.C. the divinely provided twopence. At once he rose and indicated the urgency of visiting Butler's shop. But, just as we reached the foot of the church steps, we saw before us an old woman, a stranger, and obviously a beggar; and she saw twopence in my hand. "Is that your mother's money?" she said. I said: "No"; and then, remembering a story of a good, much respected boy I had found in a book given me by the effusive Miss K., I added: "You are poor; will you have this penny?" (There *were* penny balls.) The old witch took it and remarked: "I must buy myself a bit of bread, so give me the other one too." I paled, but did. The horror and contempt of A.C. at these proceedings haunt me still at the bottom of the church steps; and Charity has never seemed to me quite as melodious as she might have done.

The notion of angels possessed me oddly in those days. One day a large roundabout was performing in the club meadow. I was all for it; but, while I was contemplating the galloping steeds ("Not half so good as Penfold's," put in A.C.), I was beautifully diverted. Above them, round the revolving canopy, there ran a series of paintings of—angels, not ineffectual ones either. One of the pictures showed a frightful chasm between two indigo mountains, over which as a bridge lay a fallen pine. A small boy with a bundle in his hand was walking across this perilous bridge. But behind him, with hands on his shoulders, was a tall pink and silver angel. There was no doubt the lucky boy would get across. But was this painting correct? I felt indeed that angels were available; clouds at sunset were very nearly angels; but in some way the actual appearance did not happen. This visionary passion waned into something tolerably prosaic— a theory of prayer. I communicated it with success to my brother G. When we went to the wicket, we silently petitioned the Deity to give us a few runs. Throwing in our lines at Two Bridges or Mill Place, we prayed for a roach or two, possibly a chub. So seldom did advantage come of these supplications that in the end a disgraceful formula was evolved. If Heaven granted the boon, we undertook not to break into the plantation on the way home; if not, we were free, and willing, to take our cherries or apples. I am not sure whether even this was the final state of the theory of prayer.

Fortunate are those children whose homes are near some pleasant half-river, half-brook; and, from my early luck,

I can always live delightfully in George Peele's verse on the bower which was

> *Seated in hearing of a hundred streams.*

It needed no classical poetry then for us to personify our many rivulets; they, like the dogs, the butterflies, the birds of the village, "had a purpose, and their eyes were bright with it," where they hurried round the black-green stones and twinkled over sand and mother-of-pearl shells. Now we saw just one being, now a host of fairy-like creations. The Beult was not itself, though, where it formed the sombre pool under Cheveney sluice-gate. It only passed through that prodigious pit, to my feeling, and was glad when it was by. Of the depth, the inhabitants of that pool, we were zealous imaginatives. Under frosty stars the mill-keeper said to my friend, his son, as the roar of waters grew on our hearing over the low ground, that the pool in flood would be 60 feet deep. The pool in summer noon revealed big steely-blue chub; we could see their designed scales through the crystal shell of the surface; and our imagination mingled with realities. For, at such a time, Will B. pulled out a bream, and what a bream he looked to us! "Mother!" shouted he, and she came hurrying from putting out her linen on the palings of the cottage garden. She looked at the fish dangling from his important hand, and mildly disagreed with his assertions—"No, not three pounds, Billy; five or six ounces." When we considered the bream again, he *did* seem to be nearer her account of his size; but there were still others in the pool which would one day answer all our fancy, and even convince her. The day has nearly receded beyond my sense, but still there is something about that pool which does not let me peep at it through the hazels without stirrings of mystery and wonder.

Parental Vagaries

OUTSTANDING MEMORIES OF AN INTERESTING CHILDHOOD centre round my father, Lord Curzon, and the methods which he adopted for educating his three daughters.

A few months after our return from India in 1905, on the termination of my father's Viceroyalty, my mother died at the age of thirty-six. I was then ten years old with a clear photographic picture of India, the Delhi Durbar, the State Ball, and other important events during my father's term of office, but with no sense of appreciation of what I had had the unique opportunity of witnessing.

In 1908 my father rented Hackwood, near Basingstoke, which was to be our home till we all grew up, and it was there, with a little more leisure on his hands—if it was ever possible to apply that word to my father—that he concentrated on improving the minds of his two elder daughters by means unique unto himself, which left indelible traces on their minds. A third daughter, nine years younger, for a time escaped the inquisition.

Day after day, at meal after meal, the events of history

27

were drawn for us in graphic thrilling portrayal by my father, cloaked in the superlative English he always employed, pulsing with reality and life, as if they were mirages in front of our very eyes, to fade a few moments later for yet another to replace the previous vision. It was up to us children to guess those incidents and the governess had also to compete.

As I look back on those lunches and dinners I realise that my knowledge of history is largely built up on those vivid pictures more poignantly sketched than by any history book. But at that time the sense of appreciation was considerably dimmed by the sick feeling at the pit of one's stomach, one would fail to guess the occasion described—causing the food to stick in one's throat.

I can recollect a long line of perturbed governesses getting nerve-wracked themselves in this persistent fusillade of guessings and questionings which frequently left them stranded, looking utterly ignominious as so-called perfected instructors of the young. Our only response in facing defeat was the eternal phrase: "We have not got as far as that." My father always replied that we had never moved beyond William the Conqueror.

From these agitating contests in history he deviated to lighter courses of mind-training in concealing towns, rivers, mountains, poets and authors in sentences, seeing who could detect them first. Even the local clergyman was dragged in, on his occasional visits, his face becoming purple and the veins swelling on his neck when my father asked him on what grounds he assumed Elijah was seen ascending to heaven in a chariot of fire. My father's knowledge of the Bible was the most complete of anyone I have known—tinged with amusing suggestions as to the origin of some of its legends and beliefs.

When we were not being examined on such lines, my father's relaxation took other equally energetic forms.

Returning from his arduous labours in London during the week, hours would be spent from Saturday to Monday hanging pictures on the walls on the assumption that no picture-hanger ever hung pictures straight or accurately. I can still see my father wobbling at the top of a flight of housemaid's steps, with three little girls holding on to its base, handing up, with their remaining free hands, foot-ruler, nails, hammer and cord in proper rotation to the imposing figure at the top. Dusting expeditions followed, with fluffy brilliant emerald and vermilion feathered brushes, again on the supposition that housemaids never dusted books or picture frames adequately. He also had a mania for dis-covering grubby finger marks on door panels or walls, and we were sent chasing to the kitchen for bread pellets to remove the ugly stains.

Most vividly of all in my memory stands out the plantain digging on the lawn at Hackwood. On our arrival, my father complained to the astonished gardener, secure in his post for many years, that he did not know how to keep lawns free of plantains. He would proceed to show him the correct method. Week-end after week-end three drab pig-tailed daughters would stand like sentinels round the crouching figure of their father, spiking out the plantains, leaving them to collect the roots and remains into little wicker baskets and a wheel-barrow. Before commencing on each occasion, a footman would emerge with a small rush mat for my father's right knee to kneel on, carrying the murder-ous pronged spud to break up the insidious growth of the vile weed. Sixpences rewarded us for the discovery of fresh plantains; shillings for anything so monstrous as thistles.

He went from personally selecting governesses to himself choosing a dog for his youngest child after years of suppli-cation on her part. An advertisement in *The Times* thronged the hall at Carlton House Terrace with a variety of canine species from pedigree to mongrel, the owners sometimes exceeding their animals in incredible appearance. Sitting in his study, he questioned each owner as to the reliability of the dog's habits on carpets and chairs. No aspirant to the new home had ever sinned before. But one contestant let his species down by lifting his leg on the distinguished Foreign Office bag at my father's feet. The test was too strong for succeeding dogs; they all failed miserably till a drab brown Pomeranian, with breeding of no importance, too brow-beaten and cringing to attempt such *lèse-majesté*, was purchased, through the fact that it had withstood the out-pourings of fifteen other dogs on this invaluable Foreign Office "Tester."

Compared to the bleak horror of my father's youth, dragooned by the cruel and relentless Miss Paraman, who left an indelible stamp on those brothers and sisters who came under her sway, my memories are not tainted with severity and punishment, but through them winds a golden thread, clearly discernable in a very varied tapestry, of the lasting influence my father had on the development of his children's minds.

My Grandmother's House

WHEN MY MOTHER DIED I WAS THREE AND A-HALF, AND MY sister seven. My mother was ill for some months before the end and in such a period of domestic crisis two children were terribly in the way in a small house. We were therefore transferred to the house of my paternal grandmother and stayed there, in all, for a period of nearly two years.

It was a much larger house than ours, old-fashioned, with tall stucco front, and iron balconies protruding from the first floor windows. A small patch of lawn lay to the front, and french windows opened from the back parlour on to a garden at the back, with an ivied wall, a border of "London Pride," and a somewhat bare and untended rockery.

Revisiting it after many years I was astonished by its smallness; to my childish eyes it was as vast as a wilderness and as haunted as a forest. But the most striking feature about the house, and the one which I remember best, was a spiral staircase beginning in a dark flagged passage between the two cellar kitchens and climbing steeply, the full toll of its fifty stairs, to a top landing of bath-room and box-room. Higher still was an oval fanlight, very large when you were near it, but from the bottom of the well, a tiny window divided, superfluously, into tinier panes.

The inhabitants of the house, besides us two children, were my grandmother, her unmarried sister and a protective male, who had no real existence, but whose dusty bowler hat hung permanently on the branched hat-stand in the hall for the terrifying of prospective burglars.

In the hall also hung two faded brown lithographs of "The Emigrant's Departure" and "The Emigrant's Return"; on the first floor landing an oleograph of Nelson being protected from the too enthusiastic crowd. The back-bedroom, where we slept, had a picture of swans and reeds painted over mirror glass, and on the mantelpiece a large wooden clock with a tick loud and terrifying as the strokes of fate.

The front parlour was never used, except by my grandmother when she beat upon the window in order to scare small boys from playing immediately outside our railings, and its furniture had a stiff and formal look due in part to its antique design, and in part to the dust-covers which protected the loose covers which in turn protected the upholstery of the chairs. There was a good deal of china about, including one magnificent Staffordshire jug, and we children were not encouraged to play there.

The back parlour was the living-room, and here my grandmother sat in state on a high rocking-chair fastened by springs to an immovable base. She suffered from her heart and from her legs, and, although neither of these ailments prevented her sweeping through the house like a tornado armed with a duster—if one can admit so incongruous an image—she spent a considerable portion of her time in a shiny black gown in her accustomed seat. She was much addicted to the use of homœopathic medicines, and kept a whole array of microscopic bottles of pilules always to her right hand, at a corner of the furry tasselled cloth which covered the huge dining-room table.

We children played with our toys at this table, each perched on a heavy chair with horse-hair seat and rounded mahogany back, or told one another stories in the low window seat looking out on the garden. My sister read, although a little worried by the household distinction between "Sunday books" and everyday books; *The Sunday at Home* falling into the first category, *The Leisure Hour* into the second. I was too young to be troubled with these theological questions and spent most of my time with a pair of scissors cutting figures from the illustrated papers. These figures represented, if my memory serves me, either Russian or Japanese soldiers, for that was the particular war then in progress, and I cut out so many of them that I had a permanent callosity on my second finger.

My great-aunt dwelt entirely in the basement, never emerging except to climb to her top-storey bedroom, and that of course was long after we had been put to bed. On Sunday evenings, however, she put on an embroidered black cape and a bonnet with a feather and went to church, for she was a staunch churchwoman of the Evangelical School. The rest of the family was Nonconformist, and my great-aunt's worship was always something of a mystery to our infant minds. In her leisure moments, which were not many, she read the Bible or Adam Clarke's commentary thereon, and this in spite of the fact that Clarke was no churchman, and in his day, regarded as heretical, on account of his firm

33

opinion that Satan tempted Eve not in the shape of a serpent, but in the guise of an ape.

If my grandmother was the Government in the house, my great-aunt was the Opposition. My grandmother was all aggressive energy; she all passive resistance. She nearly always won. Disputes on questions of domestic management were conducted by shouts from parlour to kitchen and back again, and when they were over my grandmother would thump herself with a clenched first to dissipate the wind which had gathered about her heart. We children were always half awed and half delighted by this performance, and with the unconscious cruelty of youth would ask her to "do it again."

I dreaded bedtime, for it meant climbing fearfully up the haunted stairs, and passing through the horrible dark landing between the bedrooms. Even Nelson looked sinister after nightfall, and the harmless aspidistra on the landing table was a nameless horror. Fortunately, I slept with my sister, and, in her comforting company, even the clock of destiny gave a tolerable tick. I was entirely under her influence and my imaginative life therefore had a feminine bias which lasted until I went to school. In bed, before we went to sleep we would play at being ladies. Sometimes for a treat we allowed ourselves to wear evening dress, which meant undoing the necks of our nightdresses and pushing them down over our shoulders—an idea borrowed, no doubt, from some chance picture in an illustrated magazine of the 'sixties. Sometimes my sister would recite, in a low voice, the opening lines of *Marmion* or Longfellow's *The Children's Hour*, and these two poems have had a magical significance for me ever since. Even now I can raise a delicious shudder at the lines:

> Do you think, O blue-eyed banditti,
>   Because you can scale the wall,
> Such an old moustache as I am
>   Is not a match for you all?

34

Moustache and Banditti! Potent and incomprehensible words! What wonder has been lost to me since you slipped into your proper perspective!

In the morning it was understood that my sister should help me to dress, and this she did willingly enough until my fifth birthday. Then she announced, with irritating calm, that she would do so no more, and I was left with the apparently insoluble problem of inserting two small legs in one pair of knickerbockers. At last I had an inspiration, and, placing the garments flat on the floor, lay down beside and slowly wriggled myself into them. It was the end of my infancy.

A week later my father set up a new establishment, with a distant relation to keep house for him, and we left my grandmother's for ever.

Those
Elfin Days

CHILDHOOD STANDS OUT FOR ME AS A TIME OF INTENSITY of perception and of thought.

From the haze of the retreated past, recur scenes poignantly vivid, pulsating with a life as of fire.

In Potter's Park,[1] now obliterated by dull buildings, the sun blazes from a sky, blue, cloudless, vibrant with excitation. On the grass, piercing green, rolls the white ball of the nurse's knitting. I stoop to catch it, and raise my eyes to a vision of lovely youth; through the glamorous mists of dazzling sunshine my uncles advance as young Gods, treading the magic sward. . . .

Ah! never again are skies so fair as those of childhood. The larks soar upward into the limitless light, with the song which pours forth rapture; everywhere birds singing melodious

[1] Manchester.

36

notes, everywhere beauty; great stretches of sunlit grass, great stretches of shadow; oaks rugged and strong, beeches, the smooth grey bark of their mighty trunks caressed by tender leaves; everywhere flowers, even of grasses and tiniest weeds, tinted and patterned with exquisite delicacy; sources of joy and discovery unending.

How pleasant to wander in the hayfields, with high ox-eye daisies, tangles of purple and golden vetches and lilac scabious. Handfuls I gathered, to note their limitless variety. Then, under a group of towering elms, or on some hillside, realised suddenly the infinite smallness of the little blossoms, and of myself in the immensity of the rolling country, field upon field of waving grasses.

Days were long then, with vistas of thought, calm and tranquil. In the woods the scent of the earth and the trees, the gracious harmony of shape and shade were imbued with a friendliness serene, which laid filaments of soothing sweetness upon the tired mind. Yet, even here, the pent yearning to express the joy surging within made rapture pain.

In the murky atmosphere of my native city beauty revealed itself and left its impress. Rare holidays in the country were Elysium. I always wept as the returning train carried us through the dingy approaches of the terminus.

The craving for beauty was insatiable. When illness or sorrow dimmed perception of it life seemed drear and sordid. The streets then jaded and repelled me. Memories of hot pavements float back to me; of aching little feet in shoes too tight; of people in rags, of faces pinched and hungry, of dreams which cut across the weary ugliness of actuality. . . . A water-cart, its bright spray making my parched mouth yet more thirsty, would bring to my eyes a fountain playing in a cool garden. Southampton Row,[1] dingy Theobalds Road,

[1] Near Russell Square, London, W.C. Where we went to live when I was six years old.

crowded Marchmont Street, where Susannah, our nurse, preferred to shop, were obliterated. . . . A river with irises on its marge flowed on. . . . I followed it to distant lands, where slow-moving barges were manned by swarthy sailors with golden rings in their ears. . . . Trees laden with bright fruits dipped to the water's edge. . . .

Always the goal of my dreams was a life of abundance and plenty, where poverty and sorrow should be no more.

Intense ethical struggles rent my heart. Even to-day a remorseful memory from the days of six years old goads me for a blow never dealt on a little bare buttock crawling before me. Its owner had torn and crumpled some drawing of mine, whilst I dwelt still in the sacred hopefulness of its creation, before the torrential misery of failure to achieve the inner vision had scourged me. High-hearted and engrossed, a pang convulsed me for that destruction. I intended an indignant blow at the departing mischievous one. Yet my hand failed of its purpose, compunction filled my being. The tears welled. The blow became a caress; gently I touched the soft flesh without hurt to the little brother. He crawled on heedless.

In my heart remained the wound of the blow I had thought to deal him. I wept with my head resting on the old nursery sewing machine, till my eyes saw with surprise a pool of tears. A memory crystallised for all time; for in some days the little brother lay in the throes of diphtheria. We heard from our beds a terrible wailing of our mother for her boy. Next morning Frank was but a beautiful image; as marble cold and still.

The house was hushed to silence; all laughter quenched. One's heart raged with a wild, impotent sorrow. Around me everywhere was a sad dullness. The mind was distraught by a consuming pain; one was swept by a fierce impulse to fling oneself to the earth, and yet one remained stupidly upon one's feet. Mocking voices sounded in one's ears.

One's parents had grown enormous in proportions; their sorrow loomed hugely. With awe and worship one crept away from them, or approached them from duty, yearning yet reluctant, overwhelmed by a great unworthiness, a great longing that one might die to restore to them the gay little Frank, who, to one's inner eyes, appeared so often still, clearly and brightly limned, more real than these shades of familiar things, which seemed intangible and dim!

Only my father's "We must not forget Frank!" and his warm, eloquent talk of the little brother assuaged in part the misery of my stricken heart. It was his gift to keep ever green the memory of the beloved; to maintain the heart high and the thought unsullied by the burble of common talk.

My brother Harry was born ten months after Frank died. They both were named Henry Francis. To my mother the expected infant was "Frank coming again." To me, when he came, the loveliest child that ever was. To hold him was joy; to be allowed, on some rare occasions, to share my bed with him, was rapture. I lay awake, with arms about him, holding my breath least he might wake.

My mother took pleasure in decorating her new big house in Russell Square. We children played for uncounted hours in the Square garden—to me, a realm of ever new delight.

After long years I returned to see the garden, and, lacking the keys, peered through the railings, barred out from childhood's Eden. It seemed all changed; a town-worn place of sombre growths. Yet within I think it must hold still the old glamour. Still in the round walk of the plane trees the sun pours golden through the translucent green. . . . Still smile enticing the great lawn of the daisies, the dearest of childhood's flowers, and the lawn of the white clover, frequented by humble-bees.

One summer only a long bed was planted with sky-blue

larkspur, a great bank of abundant loveliness, graced by the winged joy of numberless butterflies. It threw my mind into a turmoil of exaltation.

Next day would be Harry's first birthday. I imagined his flaxen hair and fair skin, rose-flushed through the tan, his rounded limbs, wreathed and garlanded with the flowers—and fell to plucking them. The dark little Adela babbled at my side and gathered also a huge bunch.

We hastened to the gate with our trophies. Not yet had the veils of magic fallen from my eyes. Not dimly did I realise that I had transgressed.

"For Harry's birthday!" we cried, when Susannah came to unlock the gate and take us home.

She upbraided me angrily, snatching the flowers away.

Then followed hours of gloom and misery indescribable. Bowed down by a sense of guilt overwhelming, I asked myself how I could have committed this unsocial act. None of us had ever done so dreadful a thing before!

At last I was called to my mother's bedroom. The flowers were there, menacing in their loveliness, displayed in tall vases. My knees trembled, and breath came short.

My mother spoke with unexpected gentleness. It was a pretty thought of a little girl to arrange flowers for her brother's birthday; but such things must not be. . . .

A surge of sorrow and gratitude overcame me. I fell on my knees and wept upon her hands, imploring: "Oh! help me to be good!"

That was often my cry in the storm-swept hours of childhood, when tiny sins loomed large, and the mind was as wax on which impressions were graven deep.

We did not go to school. Drawing, reading, writing, dreaming mainly filled my days, days ever teeming with thought and the heart's striving.

Our house in Russell Square was a centre of meetings and

40

conferences: for Women's Rights, the Abolition of the House of Lords, Radicalism, Republicanism, Agnosticism, Socialism, the New Trade Unionism.

Instructed by my father, the most earnest and eloquent of mentors, as to their purport, we children were eager to assist in these activities, taking the collections, distributing leaflets, listening, absorbing, seeking to know and to understand. Already one knew that before one lay a social duty.

In 1893 we returned to the city of my birth. Our parents immersed themselves in the rising movement of Labour and Socialism in the Industrial North. I was a big girl of twelve now; a pupil of the Manchester High School, enthused for Socialism, burning with pity and indignation for the dwellers in the grey and dismal slums.

At the open air meetings my warm clothes shamed me beside their rags. The dear red may trees in the garden at home, greeting the eyes on our return, seared with a sense of difference.

Agitations for the unemployed and the ill-paid, in which even a child could play her humble part, dispelled domestic jars and introspective sorrows, uplifted the mind to a high fervour. One was conscious of Society and its ills. The yearning for a golden age of universal happiness took more practical shape. One girded oneself to serve the commonweal.

Childhood had given place to girlhood.

The Fear of God

ONE VIVID RECOLLECTION OF A PAST MORE WEATHER-beaten than I would have dreamed I could (as doubtless I did) deserve, was taking tea with the late Harry Gosling. Harry was one of the most genuinely saint-like personalities I have ever met, and, knowing how well saints and stones go together in this world, I remember what a shock it gave me to hear him give expression to these remarkable words: "If I had the chance," Harry said, "I would live the whole of my life over again."

The effect of this sentiment upon me was so extraordinary that I have not only remembered his *ipsissima verba* for six years, but the intonation of voice, the placidity of temper, and the manner of smiling retrospection with which they were spoken have remained as fresh in my memory as though it were at this moment striking five o'clock on the day we drank tea together. If one of the good djinns were to offer me so abominable an opportunity, I should undoubtedly make the sign averting the evil eye, murmuring Samuel Butler's wisdom: "Always fear the Devil most when he dresses like an angel." And if the djinn continued to press his hateful magic upon me with the roguish affability of a spirit doing me the worst turn the malice of guardian-angelhood could from a supernatural ingenuity invent, my answer would be: "Sir, you are altogether too generous. Allow me with thanks to decline your handsome offer, except in one modest particular. The last month of my life hitherto I will most gladly live again, but for the years behind it, do not, I pray you, disturb their recumbent bones, nor clothe them with the gift of a resurrection I am, I assure you, very far from seeking."

"To travel back the ancient track" into the days of my "angel infancy" is not, therefore, a memorial exercise in which (dewy-eyed) I take a sentimental pleasure. My four seasons did not begin in the right order. Instead of opening in orthodox routine with shy and winsome spring and proceeding through the regulation course, they led off with the equinoctial gales of autumn through a somewhat dank winter into an unduly prolonged east wind, until I reached my June (which has rhymed with "tune" in the most mellifluous fashion I could ever have imagined possible) just about the time when in proper rotation I ought to have been thinking of October and the falling thatch. My youth, if William Blake's word is to be taken for it, appears to have just started piping down the valleys wild. My literal childhood was a grimmer, sterner, steeper business altogether. I very much prefer to forget it.

But I have one memory enshrined which can still give me a joy of purest ray serene and with which even the hanging of my sister captured by the pirate chief and cut down with her tongue hanging out, cannot compete. This notable occasion was when, before reaching my 'teens, I cursed God, but did not die. We wretched children had a Scotch Presbyterian nurse who was a good woman. She was such a good woman that she thought about nothing else but evil.

43

The holy purpose and fanaticism of her life were to put the fear of God into us, and towards this pious end she spared neither means nor pains. She whipped us with the rod of the spirit and we writhed beneath it. God has gone through a good many metamorphoses before He has reached His modern status of a supreme electrical engineer. To us He was a more infernal ogre than ever plagued us even in the worst of our nightmares. He never let us alone. This rumbling Moloch was not only present in the storm; His moral chastisement was ready to pounce upon the most trifling offences. He had a hundred eyes like Argus, a hundred arms like Briareus, and His scourge was bound with a hundred scorpions. Oh! how we hated Him, this just God, this retributive demon, this menacing, sour and bearded patriarch, this majestic uncle of the snivelling Jacob, this indefatigable shepherd who would never give His lambs a skip from the fold! But we feared Him even more than we hated Him, even more than He bored us in church.

I do not remember what incident it was which broke the cowering submission of years, but I remember exactly what happened and where it took place. One day, at any rate, I had had enough of it. With a resolve so fearful that it scared me into an almost epilepsy, I stealthily retired into the lavatory. I have forgotten why it was there I had determined to play the little Lucifer. Perhaps it was because I knew I could be alone there, and so meet my doom in private. Perhaps, too, I had some obscure and tortuous idea that for the ceremony to take place in the lavatory turned it into a kind of Black Mass. Be that as it may, it was to the lavatory I went, and, having locked the door, I stood straight, shut my eyes, and, with my arms pressed stiff to my sides, I whispered three times: "O God, I curse Thee," "O God, I curse Thee," "O God, I curse Thee!"

To my dying day I shall never forget the hideous Calvary I suffered in waiting for that thunderbolt to fall—never,

never shall I forget it. My anguish was so extreme that I was quite literally sweating with terror—I was damp all over. And nothing happened! My heart thudded on like the tom-tom of the damned and still I was alive! Gradually relief stole over me like drops of rain, and then a shower in the desert, but the reaction was so violent that my knees gave way, and I sat down with a bump on the seat. But when I stepped shakily out into the world again, it was, had I been able to analyse my *volte-face*, as the complete child-sceptic. But for days afterwards I kept my eyes skinned for any belated spite of Providence and walked with circumspection lest the ground might open beneath my feet.

Villa
Macolai

WHEN I THINK OF MY CHILDHOOD, I SEE, AS BACKGROUND
to its varied episodes, its glorious dreams of imagined
adventure, and inglorious actual escapades, a smooth, warm
blue sea curving round a fishing bay, tideless, waveless,
swaying gently up and down the shore, with a little dragging
whisper as of a soft wind in a forest. And, putting out on it,
a Rob Roy canoe containing five children, three in the
middle and one astride on each end. For thus, on a fine
summer evening, the Macaulay family was used to embark
on its daily nautical adventure to the jut of rocks half a mile
up the shore. Arrived at these rocks, the crew would turn
pirates, maroon one another, find islands and treasure, fight
for life, fling one another into the sea, overturn the craft
and sit on its backside, and finally voyage home as wet as it
was possible to be. Whether they were clad in bathing-suits

46

or in frocks and knickerbockers made no difference to the wetness, but some to the conscience, as they came in sight again of the red house on the shore.

The Villa Macolai, or Villa Inglese (so called locally, though by its owners the Villa Levante), stood so near the waves' edge that a high sea would occasionally rush into the garden and through the basement windows, making a miniature subterranean ocean that could be pleasurably navigated on boards. On either side of the house was an *orto*, full of oranges and lemons, eucalyptus and figs, and behind rose steep terraced hills, clad with pines, olives, myrtle and juniper, with stony paths winding up them. The little town lying between sea and hills had deep stone streets smelling of fish, drains and roasting coffee, and deep arches opened on to the shore, where they dried and mended fishing-nets, made rope, or built ships. My intelligent parents, compelled by my mother's health to live in Italy, had selected a place devoid of English visitors, churches, doctors and consumptives. We were, in fact, the only foreigners there. We did lessons with our parents: Latin, Italian, mathematics, etc., with our father; other subjects with our mother; except for one rather strange six months, when my sisters and I attended the local convent school.

Our neighbours were kind and charming. The shops gave us sweets and toys, and the nice old *parroco* came at Easter and sprinkled our house with holy water, and gave us lovely twisted coloured wax candles at Candlemas. There was a younger priest, probably less nice. "*Ancke troppo*," said his flock, with a shrug. Tolerant Latins, they yet preferred moderation. The *parroco* wanted one of my brothers, a beautiful child with curly hair and large, thoughtful, misleadingly innocent blue eyes, to be little St. John the Baptist and lead an unruly lamb in the annual procession of Santa Caterina da Siena, the town's patron saint. My brother, I think, was for doing this; he thought it would be fun to lead the lamb. His brothers and sisters were certainly for it; we thought it would be fun to see the lamb leading him. Our mother was for it; she thought it would be friendly to accept. Our nurse was for it; she thought he would look sweet. But my father, the only member of the household who had been to a public school, was not for it; he thought it would look silly, and vetoed it. These processions were splendid and entrancing pageants, as they wound through the narrow streets, chanting harshly, swinging incense and bearing great simpering wax saints.

Our time at the convent school was rather boring. We thought the nuns silly. I see now that they were merely actuated by the charming prudery peculiar to nuns. On the very few occasions when we joined in a school walk, the nun in charge, when men came in sight, would modestly turn down her eyes and say to her flock: "*Abbasso gli occhi.*" I do not remember if the little Italians lowered their eyes, but the little English certainly did not. I remember too my eldest sister, aged thirteen or fourteen, strolling to the window during a lesson to throw out pencil shavings, and being asked, surprisingly, if she was throwing a note to a man in the street. It may have been these things, together with the very Genoese Italian and French we were picking up, and with a belief that it was time we had an English education, that caused our parents to end our convent school careers.

But the pattern woven by memory is of those evenings playing pirates and explorers by and in the sea, or rounders and cricket on the sands; of hill walks, with my father telling us stories from Herodotus, Froissart, or the Inferno (we enjoyed those infernal circles), or my mother spinning entrancing tales out of her head; of wandering in and out of dusky, incensy churches, in which my mother could not kneel without wishing that the notice "*Vietato sputare*" were more frequently observed; of hanging about the dark little shops, with their sacks of coloured beans, long wands of macaroni, and lovely plaster madonnas, saints and cattle; of (after such visits) hunting fleas over one's person in vain (only one of us could catch these insects; it was her special gift); of chasing round garden or orto after fleeing rabbits, ducklings, goats or dogs; of sitting alone in an olive tree up the hill or in an ivy clump on the top of the orto wall, reading or writing poetry or stories (we had, fortunately, no restrictions on our reading), or spinning one's private interminable tales of perilous and heroic adventure by land and sea, while the mule carts jingled along the shore road, and the fishermen hauled in their heavy nets with loud cries of expectation and hope, and the hot sweet tang of the hill-side above mingled with that of the sea below. It was against this background that were set the ecstasies, tragedies, adventures and dreams, bewilderments, tediums, excitements and dramas that are the wild stuff of that tranquil time, childhood.

Later they took us to England and school, and we lived in a University town, where we wore shoes and stockings all day, and where, did we lapse (and we did) in the streets from respectable behaviour, a schoolfellow from the girls' High School or the boys' Preparatory was sure to pass and put us to shame. We could, and did, be Sherlock Holmes and track criminals unobtrusively (or so we hoped) in the streets; but it was a poor kind of a life.

Fear in Fancy Dress

I HAVE ALWAYS HAD A PASSION FOR FANCY DRESS. FROM the days when, as a very small child, I unpicked from their backgrounds of painted cardboard the accoutrements of a soldier or a postman, this passion made for itself a hundred occasions for satisfaction, culminating in my first sailor suit (*circa* 1907), which planted me at once in a new imaginary world.

In December, 1914, when I was just thirteen, I went to Knole as usual for the Christmas holidays. We were not a large party. My father was at the Front; my uncle at a camp somewhere in East Kent; so my aunt was left to manage the party herself. Besides my mother and sister and myself, there were only my cousins, Harold and Vita Nicolson, Harold's sister Gwen, Mrs. Walter Rubens, and a girl who was a close friend and constant visitor to Knole, and whom I will call Christine.

The weather was frightful and one day Vita and Gwen, bored I suppose by the incessant rain, said: "Let's dress Eddy up as a Persian prince."

I was of course delighted with the idea, which was also to be a surprise for Christine, who was working as a nurse in the hospital in Sevenoaks, and for Harold, who was returning from London that night; both were to be fetched by the car and would arrive half-way through dinner. I had seen the magnificent clothes and stuffs which Vita had brought back from Constantinople, and could hardly wait for dinner-time to be dressed up.

As the day wore on the wind rose in violence. I have known many storms at Knole; storms in which, much later in my life, my uncle and I sat alone shivering in the icy house and mentally counting the trees falling in the park; but the one of which I now write was by far the most violent of them all.

I cannot remember much about the clothes I was put into, except that they were richly red and yellow and purple and very heavy. At last there remained only the turban, a long piece of gauzy stuff which Vita wound round and round my head, and out into a long peak at the back.

After it had been tightly fixed, my face was elaborately painted white, with hard round discs of brilliant red on the cheekbones, and my eyes were painted round and far out into the temples with indigo. I was given masses of jewellery—ropes of pearls and great heavy gold bangles and magnificent rings for every finger.

"Don't you go and drop any of those," said Vita, eyeing her emeralds and sapphires a little nervously.

As I sat at the dinner-table I could scarcely move my arms and hands for the weight of glittering jewels; my face felt stiff and idol-like with paint; my head was weighted back by the huge turban which stuck out a foot behind me. But I was a Persian prince and perfectly happy.

The storm grew worse and worse. The noise was incredible and the long, dark-panelled room seemed to contract and expand irregularly like the heart of a dying man. We could feel the thuds of the wind battering against the house and had to raise our voices to make ourselves heard. All at once the enormous carpet, which stretched far away from the table, began to flop and flounder like a heavy sea; the draught rushed hissing round the room. My aunt began to get nervous and called for screens, which were placed all round the table, making for us a room within a room.

"They're very late," said my aunt, referring to Christine and Harold. "I hope nothing has happened to the car. . . ."

I looked at Vita and saw that she had gone very white. At the same moment the certainty of an accident took possession of my mind. It was not a premonition, but a simple statement of fact, and I knew that it concerned Christine, not Harold. I felt no anxiety, no excitement; I just knew that something had happened, as it were the memory of a long past experience.

A door opened and the wind tore round us, in spite of the screens; the candle-flames in the tall candelabra fluttered like handkerchiefs waved in farewell. The old butler Hicks came round the screen. "There has been an accident, M'Lady. A tree has fallen on the car. They are getting stretchers."

Everyone rose to their feet—except myself. I had had no surprise: besides, I was a Persian prince heavy with gold and jewels, and had nothing to do with all this. I watched the huge emerald on my forefinger flash like seawater under the blowing candles. And I am afraid I must confess that my first thought was: "This has spoilt my effect. No one will notice that I am not dressed as usual."

My mother and Mrs. Rubens rushed to the door. My aunt was trying to comfort and reassure her daughter, who had taken it for granted that her husband was dead. Seeing my mother go, I got up with difficulty to follow her, my red silk trousers billowing round my legs, the bangles jingling on my arms.

"No, darling. Stay where you are."

Soon a footman came with more news. It was Christine alone who had been in the car. She and the chauffeur (so the latter, who was hurt but in possession of his senses, had said) had got out to move a fallen branch out of the roadway; while they were doing this another tree had fallen upon them. Christine could not be found.

Then, almost immediately, a housemaid came to tell us that Christine had been found and was being brought to the house. She had been literally knocked silly and had been found wandering about among the trees. She had taken all the pins out of her hair, so that it was hanging loose about her. She was very badly hurt. . . .

My aunt and Vita hurried out of the room, and I was left alone. In my mind was an image of Christine as I had seen her some years before in an impromptu performance of "The Miracle," which we had got up in the Great Hall. I could see her dancing in a long white shift. I felt that, in spite of my mother's injunction, I *must* see Christine now.

Jangling and rustling, with my turban trembling dangerously, I tore out of the room and through the Great Hall, which was pitch-dark and humming with the din of the storm and the gravel-screech of the rain on the high windows. At last I reached the corridor down which I knew they would have to bring Christine, in order to reach the staircase which led to her room. I hid in the shadow under the banisters; the light was dim in the passage, for only one lamp was burning, at the farther end, and a lantern half-way up the staircase gave little light.

At last I heard stumbling, difficult footsteps coming round the corner of the passage. Then I saw my mother and Mrs. Rubens coming slowly along, and between them a

53

figure in a nurse's white uniform which glimmered suddenly under the light. They were half-leading, half-carrying it, and behind them hovered some other vague figures.

I stared and stared, crouched into the shadow, afraid to move lest the noise of my bracelets or the glitter of my rings should give me away to my mother. Then, as they came into the light from the stairs, I saw that the whole of the front of Christine's white uniform was splashed with an immense design of blood. I saw her head, which hung back and rolled foolishly at every step; a savage gash protruded above her right eye; her nose was squashed quite flat across her left cheek, and blood was oozing down her chin and up into her falling hair. As they reached the staircase and paused to lift and carry her, the figures in the background coming forward to help, her eyes flickered open and she looked at my mother. "Aunt Maude?" she said faintly. The procession passed out of my sight up the stairs.

I could feel the indigo tauten and enlarge the stare of my eyes; the scarlet discs on my cheeks seemed to revolve at enormous speed. I clutched at the knob of the banisters, and all the bangles jingled up my arm, and the immense emerald on my finger flashed once. "I shall never see her again," I thought. I felt horribly disgusted and overpoweringly sorry. For the first time in my life I understood what pain and death might be.

But I could not move yet; I could only see, in my imagination, a white nun-like figure staggering crazily about in the raging darkness under the great beeches of the drive—her face unrecognisable, her long fair hair released and streaming out like a flag in the hollow wind, caught and clung to by the swaying invisible branches.

From Two to Ten!

REMEMBERING. A CURIOUS PROCESS: LOOKING BACK AND reflecting, trying to recapture lost raptures of past days.

The joy, the pang, the drama of the long, long days of childhood. The unimportant looming immense, the important passing idly unnoticed.

And the great satisfactions.

I remember when I was only two and a-half years old my pride and self-importance, trotting on my own sturdy legs beside the most odd little baby-carriage shaped like a tiny victoria, with a hood (in front of the handle-bars) which could be pushed up or down—one wheel in front, two behind, and within which my sister—then of the despicable age of one-and-a-half—sat bolt upright with a belt firmly fastened round her plump little middle. We promenaded up and down the Avenue du Bois de Boulogne, my parents having taken a pretty little apartment close by in the then Place d'Eylau; there they used to ride, my father, thin and straight with a serene brow and a golden beard, my mother radiant with youth and a bewilderingly

55

dazzling snow and rose complexion, brown eyes, dark arched eyebrows and burning bronze hair. They were often accompanied by Harry White, the young diplomat, and I was as proud as a lion-tamer when I was lifted up to reach the velvety noses of their horses which I busily patted.

In the Place d'Eylau, however, there occurred a tragedy. My mother loved canaries, and had several in a cage. They used to flutter about the room, perch upon her shoulder and feed from her hands. The arrival of eggs (in wire nets lined with pink velvet) was a great excitement to us, but they all gradually disappeared except one brilliant song-bird. One day, everyone being out and our nurse sewing in a distant room, I wandered into my mother's apartment and lo! on the balcony stood the bird-cage and the bird. Oh, joy! Oh, temptation! Why should not I also tame the golden-throated creature? My little hand opened the little door amid the gilded wires; the bird fluttered and chirruped in terror and dismay. It darted out, clung for a moment to a tree-top near by, then flew away, away into the blue. It was my turn to flutter and chirrup in fright. I rushed to spread the awful news. My mother's distress and anger were acute. I was soundly scolded and shut up for ages in the pantry. I suppose no other convenient prison was available in a small Paris flat. I was heart-broken. The balcony is still there; I often pass it and look up in amused retrospection.

Thinking of being "put in the closet" recalls the stuffy mustiness of those Black Holes of Calcutta. The furious rage one usually was shaken by at the moment. The howls one tried to make as loud and unpleasantly piercing as possible; the wrench of one's arm as one was pushed into the dark, barging up against the long cashmere or silken garments of those days, so soft, so stifling. And how one stood there, hot and still, streaming with tears; how the tempest abated and the atmosphere becoming almost unbearable one began to long for the divinely cool air and joyous light outside; the

56

sobs then ceased and one waited and listened until the deliverer came and in a single second (after one's nose had been brutally blown and wiped) one was playing about quite oblivious of the past thunderstorm. I never really minded the dark, but I confess that I really felt heroic when I was sent for my mother's handkerchief upstairs in her unlighted room (we had gas in those times), and walked in alone guided only by a faint light falling from a Chinese lantern in the hall outside, and with bated breath retrieved the necessary rag of cambric to return in triumph, head held high, curls tossing.

For I had fair curls, really the colour of gold and heavens! How tangled they got, and how hard my nurse used to drag at my wretched pate, then damp a hair-brush and twist the carefully separated strands around her fattish finger until I had seven or eight neat yellow sausages hanging down my neck. The perfection of youthful hairdressing in those times. How funny the dressing was. I was really interested in my clothes, pretty white cambric affairs, embroidered or trimmed with narrow lace or scallops and, when going to a party, all in heavy guipure, cut low around the neck, without sleeves, and with pale blue satin bows tied on each shoulder (I remember the cold, scratchy fingers of poor Nana thrust between the shoulder-strap and my warm little shoulder and the delicious slipping of the satin against my skin). A broad satin sash was also tied about my middle with a huge bow behind. I liked my sash high; my mother liked it low; I used to hate her pulling it firmly down in front, below my small stomach, and fastening it securely with a jewelled safety-pin.

Very short the little dresses were, and well can I remember the discomfort of sitting on bony knees. People would lift me up on their laps and, I venture to declare, hardly any seat is as uncomfortable as a lap. There was always a disagreeable slope and insecurity about it, and the owner of the lap (or knees) would hold me so tight that when I decided that the

57

undignified position could be endured no longer, I simply stiffened myself, stuck out my legs and wriggled firmly out of their grasp, fussily pulling down my fluffy clothes which had all slipped up to under my arm-pits in the process. Cleverly done this manœuvre always succeeded.

Of course some people had watches, large gold ones, which opened when you blew upon them. Some even rang faint fairy bells if you listened very attentively, but those pleasant lures were few.

One of my most daring adventures, when bored by the dull routine of life, was to crawl under a very big bed where it was dim and dusty, where even a broom-handle failed to reach me, carrying an old newspaper with me which I proceeded to tear, to chew and to swallow! At last, surfeited with my feast I emerged reluctantly to be severely hustled into a corner and made to stand there until, to the horror of my nurse, she found me revelling in the process of picking the wall-paper from the wall. It always seemed to be more loosely pasted in the corners.

Then my mother would rush in, lovely and rustling (how delicious the sound of silken dress and petticoat), and all punishments were at an end. A marron-glacé would appear from a moiré paper-bag, and a scent of rose and violets permeate the room. We would be hurried down to the drawing-room and find a tall friend with long drooping moustachios standing before the fire and he would probably catch me and toss me into the air. No switch-back railway, no motor hurtling down-hill has ever provided the breathtaking thrill which being thrown in the air and caught again gave me in my early youth. It was an abandonment of delight and terror never since equalled. But I forget a grand game. Take an almost empty room, far enough away from grownups, a big table, also empty, set a long slippery board against it and slide down it as rapidly as possible on to a pile of cushions below, while a hideously growling beast (a companion) tries to seize you as you whizz past, tear you off your precarious perch and drag you into his (or her) cavern beneath the table, to devour you. Almost better than sliding down the banisters, or climbing high into a tree and hanging head-downwards by your knees; favourite pastimes of mine, both successfully aggravating to the elders.

I do not seem to notice now the smell of things as I did then. The uplifting tang of the sea-wind; the scent of moss in summer lanes, the almost drunken delight found in the heart of a moss-rose and the queer bitter-sad odour of ivy leaves. The divine smell of a Christmas tree, half bruised, half burnt, overwhelmed me almost as much as the glare of starry candles, the gay rainbow of streamers, toys and ribbons. And always a star or a fairy with a silver wand shone perilously on the very topmost finger of the tree which one never could attain. Like oranges in the scented orange-groves of the south which I could never reach.

Also the scent of box. My uncle had a charming old house in the later colonial style; in wood, painted white with long clap-boards outside; a high portico with a pediment adorned the front, supported by immensely high wooden pillars, large and fluted; the floor on which they stood was painted in black and white squares.

Behind this roomy house, standing amid woods and golden grass, was a garden filled with box-hedges protecting rasp-berries and roses, strawberries and syringa. We would escape from our elders, somewhat formal and serious (family prayers and grace before meals were never omitted, and no frivolous book was to be read on Sundays in that hospitable abode), and roam about the box-girdled sweets, peeping at the low out-houses once used for the negro-servants (built in wings at the side of the great house and hidden by lilac and laburnum), and finally throw ourselves down on a carpet of fir-needles burning red in a grove of evergreens, intoxicated by the scent of terebinth and resin.

Life was more old-fashioned there on the outskirts of Philadelphia than in my parent's cottage in gay and frivolous Newport, and I think I enjoyed the contrast. My uncle's large, high rooms, the floors covered with sweet-smelling Indian matting, the walls with lovely hand-painted Chinese paper (brought back from the land of the tea-makers in my great-grandfather's own sailing clippers), a wilderness of strange birds and unknown flowers; the green shutters half closed to keep out the fires of a Pennsylvanian summer; the ice tinkling in the big silver pitcher in the dining-room while the raspberries were like rosy islands drowned in a tide of yellow cream crowned by sugar snow awaiting their doom. This was all peace and rusticity.

The great ocean I crossed so often always enthralled me; as it does still, and when I recall the absurd little steamers we used to venture upon I am amazed. Intolerably small, they would seem to me now. Stuffy beyond words below and very dark. Oil lamps swinging from the beams, dead lights in the tiny cabins, where absurdly short, narrow bunks were closely shrouded in heavy rep curtains, and the water in the basins rarely ran. We could scarcely ever have the scuttles open and eleven days was the usual period it took to steam from Liverpool to New York, during the half of which I was sick.

I remember a whale, a dark grey form moving slowly through the waters, a jet of foam spouting in the air above him; I recall a distant iceberg floating idly on the greenish waves, but I was not particularly impressed by either. A glass of lemonade with ice and a long straw seemed far more important, or the smouldering end of a burnt rope hanging in a metal box on deck and used to light the men's cigars with. Men really did wear whiskers then; my father, hand-some and distinguished, wore a beard; and women wore bonnets with ribbons fastened to them, tying under their chins; even the young and pretty ones. No rug was ever anything but a plaid. I remember once in a fire being picked up half asleep and rolled in one of them to be carried from my bed to the house next door, a rough and scratchy plaid, with a fusty smell.

Those days were all before the age of bustles even. My sister and I so admired these later aids to grace that we tied newspapers into bundles and wore them sticking bravely out behind, attached to our round childish waists under our tempestuous petticoats, while I used to stuff my coat pockets with rolls of bread which I handed to the beggars in Paris, who were furious! For they wanted stones, not bread. If I can call mere dross by the name of stones? We were usually on our way to the Champs Elysées where crowds, accompanied by little pale-faced children, wandered gaily up and down; where the wet nurses, or "nou-nous" as they were called, all wore dark dresses with white turned down collars (à la George Sand!), ample capes and lace-caps trimmed with an aureole of immensely broad ribbon-loops, two long ends of which fell behind in billowing pale blue, or pink, or scarlet.

The entrancement of that sunny tree-shaded avenue none can tell. The gay little open booths crammed with tempting toys; the man with the purple and red and green toy balloons; the delicious crisp gauffres, a sort of wafer all hot and sugary, fresh from the oven. The merry-go-rounds where, in a daze of giddy delight, one wheeled round and round, the envy of the envied; last, but hardly least, Guignol and his squeaking, battering allurement. Also, moment of supreme pride! That when one climbed into a goat-cart and held the reins in one's hands alone!

But the happy day came to an end; we trotted stumpily home trying to keep up as we tugged at nurse's hand; and after bread and butter, milk in a silver mug with a funny taste, a scrub, hair tied up and solemn little prayers, we were tucked up and the wonderful moment came when, after dark in our cots, my sister and I would wait for our mother to come and say good-night.

She would dart in all frou-frou and swishing silks or velvets, her lovely face alight, her diamonds, on a black velvet band around her throat, gleaming in the half light, her bracelets clinking with the most joyous sound as she bent down. Soft lips, a scent of attar of roses and a divine content would fall on us like a benediction.

A benediction which is with me still.

SONIA KEPPEL

The Tail

TO LOOK AT MY NURSE SEEMED TO BE AS PROTECTED FROM ordinary attack as one of His Majesty's battleships. Her piqué shirt and skirt were so stiff with starch that they might have been made of armour plating. In her watchful eye was all the confidence of a born leader of nursery-maids. Yet she had two vulnerable points of which I was sadistically aware. One was a "toe" which acted as a weather-vane, presaging storm and disaster, and the other was a "tail." Most of the nurses I knew had "toes," but none of them (as far as I could ascertain) had "tails." There was something individual and distinguished about it, something in it which retrieved her from the common herd of nurses and put her on a level with the nurses of Royalty and Sir Ernest Cassel's grand-daughters. It was made of long, coarse burnished hair and its main point was that it was detachable. It "took off" to comb. On gala days, such as a birthday or a day on which I had lost a tooth without making a fuss, I was allowed to touch it and even to brush it, and on these occasions the ceremony was a solemn one.

63

My nurse unwound it from the back of her head whereon it had lain coiled like a serpent, determinedly shook it out and shut its end into the dressing-table drawer. I was given a hair-brush and told to be careful. I can still remember my pride on the occasion of my first brushing. I went to my task with the devotion of a vestal virgin. I even made the suggestion of washing my hands first. Familiarity with the rite bred slight contempt for it and subsequently my nurse's pride was hurt when she found me driving her "tail" to market. Fiendishly I used it against her as a weapon of blackmail. I wielded it over her with the ferocity of a Moujik manipulating the knout. Her life was made hell by it until my mother intervened. "Everyone wears false hair now. It is all the fashion," she comforted poor Nannie by saying, and with the rivet mended in her armour-plating, Nannie steamed ahead once more.

I bided my time.

One winter's afternoon I was banished to the night-nursery to do penance for half an hour. Nannie had discovered me slaking my thirst with her home-made recipe for chapped hands, and I was told to stay in the night-nursery "till I was good." Determined not to affect this metamorphosis too soon, I looked round the room in search of distraction and saw the tail hanging from the drawer. (In the winter, with fogs about, an extra combing was wont to take place before tea.) An idea, colossal in its daring, stabbed my brain. I tiptoed to the window, thrust it open, and looked down on the dreary square. Vague outlines of carriages and cabs passed underneath me, and from the right I saw approaching a large van drawn by two sturdy greys. Seizing the "tail" from the drawer, I brandished it aloft and flung it from me. Down, down it went, curving and doubling and writhing, as though in the extremity of fear. The driver of the dray saw it too late to avoid it. With a grinding of rusty brakes he pulled up his horses, but not before the offside grey and two offside wheels had crushed it into pulp. Slowly he descended from his perch, peered shortsightedly at the bedraggled remains, and sadly shook his head. Then he stooped and gathered them up and rang our front-door bell. Ecstatically I leaned from the window and heard snatches of his conversation with the footman. "Sorry, sir—saw it fall just too late—must've broken its back anyway, poor little dawg——"

All These I Learnt

IF I HAVE A SON, HE SHALL SALUTE THE LORDS AND LADIES who unfurl green hoods to the March rains, and shall know them afterwards by their scarlet fruit. He shall know the celandine, and the frigid, sightless flowers of the woods, spurge and spurge laurel, dogs' mercury, wood-sorrel and queer four-leaved herb-paris fit to trim a bonnet with its purple dot. He shall see the marshes gold with flags and kingcups and find shepherd's purse on a slag-heap. He shall know the tree-flowers, scented lime-tassels, blood-pink larch-tufts, white strands of the Spanish chestnut and tattered oak-plumes. He shall know orchids, mauve-winged bees and claret-coloured flies climbing up from mottled leaves. He shall see June red and white with ragged robin and cow parsley and the two campions. He shall tell a dandelion from sow thistle or goat's beard. He shall know the field flowers, lady's bedstraw and lady's slipper, purple mallow, blue chicory and the cranesbills—dusky, bloody, and blue as heaven. In the cool summer wind he shall listen to the rattle of harebells against the whistle of a distant train, shall watch clover blush and scabious nod, pinch the ample veitches, and savour the virgin turf. He shall know grasses, timothy and wag-wanton, and dust his finger-tips in Yorkshire fog. By the river he shall know pink willow-herb and purple spikes of loosestrife, and the sweetshop smell of water-mint where the rat dives silently from its hole. He shall know the velvet leaves and yellow spike of the old dowager, mullein, recognise the whole company of thistles, and greet the relatives of the nettle, wound-wort and horehound, yellow rattle, betony, bugle and archangel. In autumn, he shall know the hedge lanterns, hips and haws and bryony. At Christmas he shall climb an old apple-tree for mistletoe, and know whom to kiss and how.

He shall know the butterflies that suck the brambles, common whites and marbled white, orange-tip, brimstone, and the carnivorous clouded yellows. He shall watch fritillaries, pearl-bordered and silver-washed, flit like fireballs across the sunlit rides. He shall see that family of capitalists, peacock, painted lady, red admiral and the tortoiseshells, uncurl their trunks to suck blood from bruised plums, while the purple emperor and white admiral glut themselves on the bowels of a rabbit. He shall know the jagged comma, printed with a white c, the manx-tailed iridescent hairstreaks, and the skippers demure as charwomen on Monday morning. He shall run to the glint of silver on a chalk-hill blue—glint of a breeze on water beneath an open sky—and shall follow the brown explorers, meadow brown, brown argus, speckled wood and ringlet. He shall see death and revolution in the burnet moth, black and red, crawling from a house of yellow talc tied half-way up a tall grass. He shall know more rational moths, who like the night, the gaudy tigers, cream-spot and scarlet, and the red and yellow underwings. He shall hear the humming-bird hawk moth arrive like an air-raid on the garden at dusk, and know the other hawks, pink sleek-bodied elephant, poplar, lime, and death's head. He shall count the pinions of the plume moths, and find the large emerald waiting in the rain-dewed grass.

All these I learnt when I was a child and each recalls a place or occasion that might otherwise be lost. They were my own discoveries. They taught me to look at the world with my own eyes and with attention. They gave me a first content with the universe. Town-dwellers lack this intimate content, but my son shall have it.

Early Days

I WAS BORN AT NO. 20 CAVENDISH SQUARE. THE HOUSE has now been sterilised by generosity into a home for nurses. Though the scent of privacy has gone for ever the architectural dignity must, I imagine, remain, Gothic and Tudor, what the Americans so eloquently label "Louis," all of these disintegrate easily in the zest of reproduction, but a genuine Georgian structure defies fake and disdains disparagement. Magnificent in manner, arrogant in understatement, Georgian architecture made houses fit for gentlemen to live in and when the gentlemen became unfit they turned Regency.

20 Cavendish Square with its square hall, its magnificent staircase, the double mahogany doors, the marble mantelpieces—Greek heads braided in plaited wheat—the conservatory limiting the abundance of a single vine (as we had always gone to Scotland before the tight green grapes had turned we could never be quite sure that they were going to be purple), the courtyard beyond leading to the stables and the servants' quarters, 20 Cavendish Square was a beautiful

house. There was Newey (Mother's maid, Miss Newson) arranging banks of flowers, and Cave, until he died of drink (as most good butlers do) presiding over fate (as all good butlers must). He had the familiarity born of affection and the indulgence bred of superiority. He had also the unerring nostrils of English servants for a lady or a gentleman—that ultimate judgment which kindness cannot modify and tips can only aggravate. The "arrivistes" and the "arrivés" should start a society for the Prevention of Cruelty from Servants. Cave held the view that masters and mistresses must be humoured in their childishness and protected from themselves. Charity in any form he abhorred. It is not of such stuff that butlers are made. He liked tall handsome footmen. Mother on the other hand preferred them to be quick-witted and obliging.

There were the glorious days when mother would come up and have tea in the nursery. The preliminary tension made Nanny very cross and the nursery-maid red and flustered. A silver coffee pot full of hot chocolate preceded her arrival. Only it was not the place of a Cave footman to bring it into the nursery. If he carried it as far as the nursery landing it was already a concession.

One day mother arrived before the chocolate—

"Cave, I don't want any more of your handsome footmen. I won't have a man who knows his place."

A week later Cave announced with a chuckle:

"I've got a real ugly one for you this time. But none of your nasty ways with him."

All servants adore mother. They stay with her for ever. Later the "ugly one" became our beloved butler and married my maid.

Cave treated life as if it were an achievement of his own, which indeed it was. Only—unlike our lives—his was a complete success. One day mother came in late.

Cave: You *are* late. Lord Spencer called.

Mother (who used to hunt at Althorp every winter): Well, it doesn't matter, Cave. I'll write his Lordship a line.

Cave: You may have overlooked the fact that Lord Spencer is going to India to-morrow as Viceroy.

Mother: Cave; why didn't you ask him to wait?

Cave: I did. I said: "Here is *The Times*, the evening papers, cigars, cigarettes, a whisky and soda, a brandy and soda, a quill pen or an ordinary pen, if your Lordship would care to wait?" But he couldn't.

Mother: Why didn't you ask him to dinner?

Cave: I did. I said: "We should be delighted to see your Lordship at dinner," but he's got a family banquet.

Mother: Why didn't you ask his Lordship to come in after dinner?

Cave: I did, and his Lordship's coming.

Cave never hurried his effects.

My earliest memory (I was two and a-half) is a game of soldiers with my brother Cys. It was my first day up after a touch and go attack of double pneumonia. I had been violently sick into a beautiful vase—I can still remember the dramatic fact that it was not a basin—and I was given this treat. I worshipped my brother Cys.

The next thing I remember, though dimly, is Queen Victoria's funeral, which I saw from the lap of the Duchess of Devonshire; but I remember it only because I had an ermine coat with tails—a cut relic from mother's trousseau. The Duchess became vivid later, because she used to give me huge scarlet candles, whereas other red candles were small, and associated only with Christmas trees and birthday cakes.

Until my brother was born I hated being called "Baby." When he usurped the title it became a proud possession, to be relinquished with indignation and a bitter sense of injustice.

In the afternoon mother would drive her phaeton, and I

71

would sit next to her. This was ecstasy. Then I would play in her boudoir—which I called the "goodoir"—furious if we were interrupted and very rude to the intruder.

I adored my sister Violet, who was ten years older than I was and always angelic to me. I can remember still the intense feeling of impotent fury that I experienced each time my nurse corrected the word "sister" or "brother" into "step-sister" or "step-brother."

My main preoccupation about Heaven was the problem of the relations between my mother and my father's first wife. Which would he love best, and how would they get on together? There was no one with whom I could discuss this point and it weighed heavily upon those hour-long minutes that precede sleep. Father and mother never missed saying good-night to me, and I said my prayers to mother. God was very clear, because he looked just like father, though I knew that He must be more difficult to cajole and to convince. (Father was always a very present help in trouble.)

I loved mother's clothes. I can see now a pale green shimmer of mother of pearl, and an orange dress with touches of turquoise. During the season there were great treats lurking round the corner. A boat on the Serpentine, strawberry ices at Gunter's, the possibility that mother, having been at a Cotillon, might have left some trophy—a paper sunflower, for instance, with bus-tickets stuck in the middle (by my governess)—at the bottom of my bed.

In the winter we went to Oakham or Manton to hunt. My beautiful white pony, Pansy (given me by my uncle Ribblesdale), could be ridden or driven—I was sometimes allowed to drive her alone—and there were the two carriage horses, Butcher and Baker, and the four hunters, Comedy, Havoc, Fireworks and Gordon, all of which we fed on Sundays with carrots and sugar. Gordon, who was over seventeen hands, jumped each nettle as if it were a hedge, caracolling like a horse in a bad picture. There was, besides, the glory of mother's prowess and the strange horses on which friends and dealers delighted to mount her.

Twice a week cardboard boxes of flowers arrived addressed to me (flowers were my great passion) and each year on my birthday there was a servants' ball in the Town Hall. It was at this time that the figure who dominated my youth came upon the scene: my governess, Fräulein Heinsius.

I was a passionate child with an extremely violent temper, biting, kicking and scratching the nursery-maids. Intense, though belated, remorse would follow. Adoring Fräu, rows were an essential ingredient of our daily diet. She had—still has—a dominant personality. Lovely grey-green eyes with long lashes, an apricot skin, a will of iron, little erudition —in the academic sense of the word—but a capacity for teaching anything, that genius for imparting which has so little to do with knowledge. Materialistic, with an ethical but never a spiritual approach to a problem, lacking some- times in sensibility, but abounding always in gusto, absolutely devoted and infinitely adventurous, she made both life and every-day life dance to her tune. She loved crowds; she loved events, the turbulent mess of life was her element. If it was impossible to get in anywhere you would find her in the first row; if there was a street accident, she would have seen it. If she never saw a murder it is murders that are discredited. She had an unerring instinct for being in at the birth and in at the death.

I was her own ewe-lamb, but she was very severe with me. I was never allowed to be pleased with myself. Always some depressing refrain would follow: "Denke nicht etwa das Herr—Dich amusant findet. Direkt langweilig findet er Dich."

Life at Manton was very regular. Mother with her two pin- cushions—one covered with brooches and the other with rings—open joys that left the secrets of her jewel cases intact, mother, exquisitely small and erect on her horses, relapsing

73

after tea into some lovely tea-gown; the oatmeal bags squeezed into the hardness of the bath water, the walks with Fräu, which only became exciting when small white violets began to lurk in the ditches.

Two things worried me: that Fräu should not call mother by her Christian name, and that she shouldn't have more furs and more jewels. If I were given any myself I always wanted to pass them on to her. When Christmas or her birthday came I would beg mother to give her a ring or a bracelet, a chain or a boa (which mother, the most generous of women, always did). Obscurely, I saw social injustice in terms of the superfluous. I couldn't bear Fräu to forego the unnecessaries of life. Youth, thank God, will always retain a jewel-standard.

Fräu had two umbrellas, "der gute" and "der schlechte Schirm." Occasionally I was allowed to borrow "der schlechte"—an unchosen responsibility imposed by the weather.

She also had Ahnungen* and, though she hardly believed in God, He always backed her up, losing the bag she had not wanted me to take, or spotting the dress she had not wanted me to wear.

The great day of the week was Wednesday. After eating bread and cheese and hot chocolate at 10.30, I was allowed to drive my pony cart into Oakham. Then the dancing class —a black accordion-pleated dress with green or scarlet shoes and stockings—and luncheon with Lord and Lady Manners, where there was always icing sugar instead of ordinary sugar. A French lesson with Francis Manners and his governess in the afternoon, would put Fräu in a good temper, because I liked my lessons and Francis didn't. After tea a rehearsal of "Athalie et Joas," which was a pleasure to me, as there had been a time when I was only Joas, and now I had become Athalie. Then home in the open pony-cart with the winter sky yielding up the Big and Little Bear.

A fragment.

* Ahnungen : forebodings, premonitions.

Talk of
the Devil

WHEN I BEGAN TO SEARCH BACK IN MY MEMORY FOR something that made the most vivid impression on me as a child, two things flashed to my mind, both connected with the Devil—the Vicar and Mr. Gladstone.

The Devil—horns, hoof and tail—was a very real personality in the sort of household I was born into nearly sixty years ago.

He was still used by nurses as a bogey to terrify children into obedience. Quite trivial offences natural to all children might draw down his appalling wrath, and the most vivid pictures were presented to us of hell with its flames and torments and lake of brimstone (which, since we had it as medicine, we could quite well believe was a Satanic product). I suppose all this has now gone by. Nurses do not now frighten young children with tales of a Devil, who is openly scoffed at in the newspapers, or a Hell, which has been airily wiped away by a new generation of Deans.

At any rate I know that many a raid on jam-cupboard or orchard, and many a minor fib to avoid hurting one's parents of the sort that in grown-ups is called "tact," were prevented by the lively fear of instant retribution from the watching Devil or the only slightly less terrible and equally ubiquitous God. God, I remember, had "an awful eye" which was constantly watching us children from somewhere in the nursery ceiling, and, in fact, the whole business was very uncomfortable.

I was taken regularly to Church, and one week it was announced that the old Vicar was retiring, and that a new one would take his place the following Sunday. There was considerable discussion between my father and mother at the family dinner table on our return from Church as to the new appointment. Listening in silence, as all good children were taught to do at the table, I gathered that whereas the old Vicar had been estimable or Low, the new Vicar was reported to be very High, and addicted to practices bordering suspiciously on the Romish and Papistical.

At that time religious controversy was particularly acrimonious owing to the new "High" influences which were stirring up the Anglican Church, and as my family were very Low I understood that the new Vicar was really little better than a Roman Catholic.

Now Rome was the Scarlet Woman of the Seven Hills in those days, and anyone who believed its pernicious doctrines was delivering himself over to the Devil as an easy prey. All that week my young mind was darkened with the thought of the approaching Sunday, but on the morning as I was being dressed to go to Church as usual, strength came and I revolted. I lay down and screamed and kicked, refused to have my coat put on, and eventually dissolved in floods of tears. It was hours before it was elicited from me by alternate smacking and coaxing that I had pictured in the pulpit a living embodiment of the Evil One with blazing eyes and lashing tail, ready to carry us all off to torment.

The new Vicar was I believe, a most excellent man and very likely rose to an Archidiaconate in the fullness of time, but I never really sat comfortably under his ministrations.

And so it was with Mr. Gladstone. My family was very staunchly Tory. The man Gladstone, who, I have learnt since then, was regarded by many as a great and good statesman of unimpeachable integrity and unswerving patriotism, was believed by them to be a Devil, and I frequently heard my father, with fist emphatic among the jingling breakfast-cups, describing him as such, when the morning paper revealed some fresh enormity of Gladstonian duplicity.

I can never see a picture of the eminent statesman even to-day without a shudder of horror. But then I feel that when I look at the pictures of most eminent statesmen.

Those were the days of real political controversy. This generation has lost the art of good hating. We have tiffs and squabbles and "coolings of the atmosphere" in politics, but no good, hearty, roaring feuds splitting the nation into halves. It is all of a piece. The prize-ring has padded its iron knuckles with gloves till one wonders whether the knuckles inside have gone soft. I wonder how Phil Scott would shape in a rough house with Jem Mace, or how a suave and gentlemanly debate between two of our modern front benchers would sound to Disraeli and Gladstone.

When topical songs were sung at the theatre in Brighton the verses about Mr. Gladstone were hissed and hooted, those about "Dizzy" were clapped and cheered. To-day topical verses in cabaret and revue are less forcibly written and raise no expressions of ardour or disgust whatever.

Incidentally the theatres and music halls have always been intensively Conservative. I cannot recall ever hearing an anti-Conservative song on the British halls. This is very interesting, but the discussion of the reasons would lead me too far from the recollections of childhood to enter into the scope of this book.

Some Children
in the 'Sixties

ONE OF MY EARLIEST RECOLLECTIONS IS OF MY FAMILY
going to a children's fancy ball given in the year 1858 by
Queen Victoria. I was not included in the invitation, as too
young, which offended me, and the little cap I was allowed
to try on was no consolation. But I thought the gold stars and
crescents which decorated my sister's plaits very beautiful,
as also the green-embroidered jacket of her Greek dress.
Though only four years old, I was taken with the others to
a children's ball at Frogmore given in 1859 by the Duchess
of Kent. It was a doubtful pleasure for me as I soon became
so tired that I lay down on my mother's train and went to
sleep. I thought it cruel when I was roused to dance with the
Prince Consort, and I remember my difficulty in reaching
his hand to try and make an arch high enough for the
country dance couples to pass through.

My only other recollection of the Prince Consort is when once on a Sunday walk with my father we met the Queen and the Prince near Herne the Hunter's Oak, in the Windsor grounds. This tree had a large hollow in the trunk, where the ghostly hunter was supposed to hide. The scene is impressed on my memory by an encounter between the Queen's dogs and our collie, though luckily they did not actually fall to fighting. Our collie was clever, and devoted to my father; but was too jealous and nervous to be safe with children. One day, irritated by our games and screams, and I the unfortunate child in his way, he planted his eye-teeth in my arm and then, terribly ashamed, ran away and hid under my bed. Our governess took him to his kennel, tied him up, and whipped him. Later in the day my sister Mary, then a very small child, was missed. At last in the backyard two small legs in white socks were seen peeping out of Skye's kennel into which she had crept to console him. My bite meanwhile was drastically rubbed over with caustic, and I can still feel the pain of this treatment, and hear my family reminding me of the extreme probability of hydrophobia. Luckily, I escaped this sequel, but the scar I have still.

One year we went to Sandown in the Isle of Wight to recover from the effects of measles. We used a funny old bathing-machine with a canvas hood over the steps, which was pulled into the sea by a horse. Here one day while taking our dip in a rather heavy surf, a wave knocked my mother down and Mary, a slippery naked baby in her arms, was swept away. Our nurse, fully dressed, had to rush into the sea to rescue her.

The winter of 1860 was bitterly cold and the Windsor skating pond was flooded and frozen. Chairs on runners were used by the elders and pushed by those who were learning to skate. It was my first experience of ice, and my front teeth— luckily first ones—were knocked out by a fall. One tooth which was only loosened I swallowed later and my family assured me that it would grow into a horn like a unicorn's. I fully believed this, and every morning looked anxiously to see if there was any sign of the horn growing out of a small scar I had on my forehead.

Mary was my junior by nearly four years. She was a fearless, independent child, and would never willingly be excluded from any of our pastimes. She took her own line with energy and determination. At a very early age she horrified our grandmother by fishing in the Slopes at Windsor accompanied by a cherry-cheeked French girl and the page-boy, and provided with a rod and a pot of worms. Grandmama, thinking that Mary threaded her own worms, called her "Little Nero, little Caligula." Indeed, she disapproved of us all, and talked disparagingly of our "brick-dust cheeks." There was not much love lost between her and us; we grudged our mother's attentions to her while she, no doubt justly, thought we were badly spoilt.

Mary once defeated the authorities by refusing to acknowledge punishment. She had picked some forbidden flowers for which our nurse had made her wear on her hands a pair of small white calico bags tied securely round her wrists. As these could not be hidden, Mary braved it out. She flourished her white bags in everyone's face declaring they were "so comfortable and so cool," pretending to feel great pride in her unusual gloves.

Our schoolroom in Windsor Castle, over the Norman gateway, had once upon a time been a State prison, and its stone mullioned windows were low and deeply embrasured. One day Mary, thinking to get her way with our governess if she could cry, but finding that no tears would come, jumped on to the window-sill, and standing up suddenly bumped her head with intention so severely as to bring the desired tears to her eyes.

My father took us one day for a picnic to Virginia Water. Suddenly he missed Mary, and saw to his horror in the distant middle of the lake, a small boat, a pair of sculls and a mushroom hat. Always nervous about accidents he started in pursuit, and as he rowed up alongside he found Mary quite undaunted, singing loudly: "Paddle your own Canoe."

When I was young, education for girls of the leisured class was decidedly indifferent. Governesses were chosen for their refinement and high principles, not because they were qualified to teach. Our discipline passed in turn from a small Hanoverian virago to an ignorant English girl who could not even keep order.

"What's the matter with Miss Harcourt?" my elder sister Victoria and I asked Mary one morning. "She's cross and says we know why," Mary sniggered. It seems she had crumbled biscuits into Miss Harcourt's bed, who, in consequence, had passed a miserable night. This sort of behaviour was no doubt a reaction from the over-severity of Fräulein Rebentisch. She, I believe, eventually became insane— because of Prussia's annexation of Hanover it was said.

It seems strange that we who were idolised by our parents, and indeed much spoilt by them, should never have told them how unhappy we were with our Fräulein. I suppose we took it for granted that governesses were immovable institutions and fancied that if we complained we should suffer for it afterwards. At any rate we said nothing though once an elder sister Victoria was made to walk for miles with a broken chilblain on her heel, and Mary, learning to read, was often battered and pinched until her poor little arms were pulp. I remember feeling like murder, and clenching my hands with suppressed rage until the nails ran into the palms at this ill-treatment of my sisters. It must have been bad for us to hate as we did then. So miserable were we that Victoria used to pray to die in the night; I used to pray that Fräulein might die!

The casual question of an uncle as to how we liked our governess finally brought about our deliverance. Startled

81

by the answer he received, he went straight to our mother about it and she, horrified at his disclosure, sent the lady off to mourn the Hanoverian dynasty at home.

Victoria was eighteen months older than me, yet we were given the same lessons to learn. I remember my difficulty in mastering our daily task of three verses from St. Paul's Epistle to the Hebrews, which Victoria repeated with correct precision. I could not understand a word, and no one ever attempted to explain the meaning of what was far too difficult for a child of my age to take in. Even the few verses which remain in my memory, such as: "God, who at sundry times and in divers manners spake in time past unto the Fathers by the Prophets, hath in these last days spoken unto us by His Son," I remembered more by the rhythm than the meaning. Further on in the Epistle I was completely lost, and yet our little German tigress expected and exacted a literal recitation of each parrot-learned verse.

We were made to get strings of dates by heart. We quite believed that the world was created in 4004 B.C., while we repeated with conviction the exact dates of Nimrod, the Babylonian captivity, and Alexander the Great. Alaric, King of the Goths, and Attila, King of the Huns, seemed to us a mysterious pair of twins on a par with Romulus and Remus. I cannot believe that a string of supposed facts was of the least use to us, and yet we plodded daily through three new dates, steeple-chasing over centuries, until we finally reached the accession of Queen Victoria.

"Upper School"

FOR THIS INCIDENT OF MY EARLY YOUTH I WILL PROBABLY be accused of disloyalty to my old school. If such a true account is disloyalty, then I am guilty. But I ought in justice to Marlborough, to say that the custom I have here described has now been abolished. Although "Upper School," with its many inhabitants still exists, I believe that its autocracy is altogether altered for the better. This account may seem to my contemporaries highly coloured. I merely describe it as it struck *me*. But then I was an unpleasant little boy, morbidly sensitive in some matters and "highly strung."

I never liked Crossman and I am sure I should not like him if I were to meet him now. He oiled up to the Bishop, who was the school "Visitor." He did his prep. without the aid of a translation. He was a great pet with some of the masters. When he left school and went to Cambridge he was a great lad at the Palais de Danse, and had a topping little two-stroke motor-bike. The money that was supposed to be training him for Holy Orders he spent on morning coffee at a dashing Cambridge Café. Somehow his was always the jolly face that greeted me when first I returned from the holidays. "Bad luck, Betjeman, you're still in Boggins's form." And he, knowing Boggins, knew what awful bad luck it was, and grinned. Characteristically he was the first person to bring me the most terrifying piece of news I have ever had in my life. "They're going to put you in the basket to-night, Betjeman."

For those who have not been through "in-college" life at Marlborough shortly after the war, I must explain what "putting in the basket" means. There are six senior in-college houses, and thirty-five boys from each, the toughest and the youngest, live during the day, in an enormous barn-like structure called "Upper School." It is about as large as the Horticultural Hall. It smells of old biscuits and bat oil, and is lined with desks, save at one end, where there is a clearing that the bloods may play indoor hockey. The bloods have double desks, chaps like me have small ones. If your desk is "unflush" during prep., that is to say, so full of books that it will not close down properly, you are publicly beaten by a boy, known as a "captain," when prep. is over.

Marlborough is a cold place, hundreds of feet above sea-level and in beautiful downland country. In Upper School there are two fires. One is known as "Big Fire." Four captains, chosen entirely because they are good at games, are allowed to sit here and the four captains choose about a dozen other boys, also good at games, to sit with them. The other one hundred and seventy boys crowd around the other fire, known as "Little Fire," or sit on hotwater pipes in those parts of the school to which they are allowed access.

"Big Fire" rules Upper School. It is true that a master comes in twice a day to take prep., but otherwise no person in authority enters the place. "By the boys for the boys"— that's the rule and with it all the advantages of communal life. Sometimes one house is not represented at "Big Fire," and suffers accordingly. My house was bad at work, bad at games and not keen on the O.T.C. It was not represented at "Big Fire," and not very keen on it.

The most fearful disgrace which Marlborough can thrust you into is the basket. Your friends desert you. It only happens a few times a year, but it is as bad as expulsion. In after-life Marlburians chatting about old times in the bars of local golf clubs will say: "Oh—Betjeman!—not much of a chap. He was put in the basket, wasn't he?" It is in the power of that tough autocrasy, "Big Fire," to put you in the basket.

This is the process. There are two large wastepaper baskets in the Upper School. During the half hour after 6.30 tea, before "prep." begins, "Big Fire" (with the captains watching at the door) comes in and seizes the victim. His clothes are taken off save his shirt, and he is thrust into one of the baskets, filled with apple cores and wastepaper, by the fags. Sometimes ink, sometimes paper and sometimes only obloquy is poured on his head. He is allowed to remain on exhibition until just before prep. begins, when he is allowed to go and "stamped out" of the building. When he returns to prep., the master in charge asks why he is late. "Put in the basket, sir." The master nods. It does a fellow good. He has probably been suspected of thieving or worn coloured socks before he had been in Upper School three times or . . . never mind. Boys know each other best. There is nothing like the moral indignation of someone who is fifteen or sixteen. Besides the fellow was unpopular.

I disliked Upper School so much that I used to keep my books in a basement where they cleaned the boots. When Crossman told me that I was to be put in the basket, I felt too sick to make a gay retort. I can see his smug figure now, as he went off to morning work, his preparation done, his clothes shiny and patched by some loving mother in a rectory. All that day I could do no work. Put in the basket. I tried to think of what I had done wrong and remembered too much. I tried to be cheerful. I distinctly saw two boys in my house standing talking and looking at me. When I passed a group I thought I heard my name mentioned. In the hall I could eat nothing. The afternoon came and evening prep. was nearer. Then came 6.30 hall. No one ate much. There was a lot of talking. "Someone's going to be basketed. . . . I say, Betjeman, someone's going to be put in the basket." When the master in charge of the hall let us go, there was a rush to the doors and across the court to Upper School. Even the greediest left his eating. There was no escape. If "Big Fire" did not catch me to-day, it would to-morrow. I got up and walked slowly across the dark gravel to Upper School. The same smell of old biscuits and bat oil was there. The gas lights were on. But there was a listlessness and excitement everywhere.

Inside, boys were walking down the alley-way between the desks. At one of them someone was sitting and pretending to read *The Autocar*. People passed by, as if by accident, just to catch a glimpse of his face. But no one came near him.

"It's Pringle." So it wasn't me after all. I felt I had better wait to see if the glorious news were true. They might be going to put two of us in. At five to seven, "Big Fire" came in. Popington, an enormous fellow, as red as beef with a tiny head, and Spewett, a boy like a cod, and a "cert" for a forty-cap next year, whom I never wish to see again, were followed by six or eight satellites. They walked straight up to Pringle and took hold of him. He offered feeble resistance. They took off nearly all his clothes. Then a pot was fetched, and he was smeared all over with red paint. We stood on desks and in clearings craning over each other's shoulders, watching in silence. An infant prodigy near me who was always a good little boy, gave a skip of self-righteous delight because he was not being put in himself. There was no noise now except the creak of the basket.

"Big Fire" hoisted it with Pringle in it on to a table that had been placed on a desk. We could just see Pringle's brown eyes through the slats. "Big Fire" stood around, smiling knowingly or looking official, ready to give the basket a stir if it were needed. Just before prep. started, and the captains came in beating their canes on the desks for the fags to start cleaning up the floor, Pringle emerged. We stamped as he walked out, a bedraggled figure, carrying his trousers on one arm, and in his hand a pair of very pointed black shoes.

What I wore
in the 'Nineties

ONE OF THE LIVELIEST MEMORIES OF MY CHILDHOOD IS
that of the clothes that I wore. That is probably because ever
since I can remember anything I always noticed the colour
and shapes of people and their clothes. There was a battle
that raged year after year between myself and my parents
about the kind of clothes I should wear. How I envy the
children now. One went to the beach to paddle in a
cotton dress, two petticoats, and goodness knows what
else. These garments were tied up in a bundle round one's
middle and one was then allowed loose to build sand castles,
to feel appallingly hot and uncomfortable, and a perfect
fool.

The first garment I was conscious of wearing was the white
vest in which I was photographed at Saltash. That was in
1891 when I was one year and eight months old. This I was

quite pleased with. I believe that on more than one occasion I descended into the dining-room of my grandparents' house during a dinner party thus attired. At York I wore a white embroidered dress. In this garment I was carried in the arms of my nurse one evening to watch the present King and Queen driving through the city when they were on their honeymoon in 1893. The crowd cheered as they passed. I waved my handkerchief, and when I got home I wept bitterly because someone had stolen my two silver bangles from my arm. After York I returned to Tenby, and, on attaining the age of four, was forced into black woollen stockings as my grandmother said that socks at my age were indecent, and that everyone would stare at me when I went out. I was taken out in a yacht by the local ironmonger and his brother, and howled for one hour with the terror of being seasick. I felt very much ashamed of myself afterwards as I was not sick at all. One day my family thought that I would look well in a boy's Eton collar attached to a stupid flannel blouse. I thought differently as the blouse was hot and the collar cut my throat. The rude boys of the neighbourhood laughed at me and I was furious. It ended in an awful scene with the collar, myself, my father, my mother and the nurse. There was not much left of the collar. This scene took place in Belfast where the street children were more cheeky and familiar than they were in England. After a time I learnt their technique of insulting other children, and got so proficient at it that I could get myself out of any situation.

When my father was stationed at Chatham, I was six or seven at the time; I was still furious that I had not been born a boy, and whenever I got the chance I would wear a sailor suit with long trousers belonging to my brother. This, of course, had to be worn in the house, for if I was seen in the garden the whole family would have the unenviable reputation of being eccentric and consequently immoral. One day a brown dress was made for me. This I did not mind, but when a close-fitting Dutch bonnet with ribbons to be tied under my chin was produced I was horrified and ashamed. We were taken to tea at the dockyard. I had a friend where father was stationed there, and they lived in one of the old ships of the same date as the *Victory*. After tea we played games with the sailors, and I could have screamed with rage, as I felt such a "mug" in my ridiculous bonnet. At Chatham I was allowed to choose a party dress. Leg-of-mutton sleeves were on the wane, and large balloon-like ones were coming into fashion. I chose Royal purple stuff and the dress was made with huge sleeves. The cuffs and the yoke were of cream coloured satin covered with lace. The effect of the lace and satin somehow reminded me of the cream buns that we ate on the rare occasions when we came to London and visited the Stores. The first party to which I was invited and when I wore the purple dress, ended in disaster. I was so pleased with my appearance and became so unbearable that another child attacked me, and it ended in a free fight where I was rescued by my nurse, taken home and whacked.

The Marseillaise

WHEN I WAS A LITTLE BOY I DETESTED MUSIC. THE PLAYING of the piano, or the voice of a trained (which means over-trained) singer, drove me frantic.

One night I awoke in a Belgian town, and heard voices singing and a band playing. They were rough voices, and they were roaring with all their might a song whose vitality and glorious rhythm made me sit up in bed to listen instead of stopping my ears. The longer I listened the more amazed I became that such an effect could be created by music. When the tune was repeated I longed to fix it in my memory; in fact, I wanted to jump out of bed and follow the crowd, adding my own little voice to the magnificent uproar. The music came nearer, until it seemed to be under my window. Unable to control my excitement I called out for my father, who was in the next room.

"What is that tune?" I asked.

"That," said my father, "is called the Marseillaise. It is the finest song ever written."

And he went over to the window and joined in the singing, beating time with his arm.

"Europe," he said, "was remade to that tune."

Of all my memories of music that remains the most vivid. It is through the window of that room in Belgium that I look at the young French officer as he plays his new song to Mayor Dietrich in the drawing-room at Strasbourg; at Mireur, singing it at Montpellier; at the men of Marseilles shouting it as they drag their guns in the blazing heat along the dusty road to Paris. Through that window, and into the darkened room, come the voices of 10th August, 1792, with the tocsin singing; all the noise of the streets. I am still sitting up in the bed, trembling with excitement, when Dumouriez sings it by the Haine, and Hoche at Wissembourg, and the young Napoleon himself on the way to Italy.

What a song!

The Curse of the Horse Race

(Written at the age of 7 years 1 month.)

Chapter I

BETTING

I BET YOU 500 POUNDS I'LL WIN. THE SPEEKER WAS RUPERT a man of about 25 he had a dark bushy mistarsh and flashing eyes.

I shouldnot trust to much on your horse said Tom for ineed he had not the sum to spear.

The race was to take pleace at ten the folowing morning

Chapter II

THE RACE

The next moring Tom took his seat in the gront stand

while Rupert mounted Sally (which was his horse) with the others to wate for the pistol shot which would anounse the start.

The race was soon over and Rupet had lost. What was he to do could he do the deed? Yes I'll *kill* him in the night, he though

Chapter III

THE FIRE

Rupert crept stedfustly along with out a sound but as he drew his sword it squeeked a little this awoke Tom seasing a candle he lit it just at that moment Rupert struck and sent the candle flying

The candle lit the cuntain Rupert trying to get away tumbled over the bed Tom maid a dash for the door and cleided with a perlisman who had come to see what was the matter and a panic took place.

Chapter IIII

EXPLAIND

While Tom and the peliesman were escaping through the door Rupert was adoping quite a diffrat methard of escape he puld the matris of the bed and hurled the it out of the window then jumed out he landed safe and sound on the matris then began to run for all he was worth

Now let us leave Rupert and turn to Tom and the peliesman as soon as they got out Tom told the peliesman what had hapend.

Chapter V

HOT ON THE TRAIL

"See there he is" said Tom "We must folow him and take him to prizen" said the peliesman.

Theres no time to spere said Tom letts get horses said the peliesman so they bort horses and and galerpin in the direcion thet had seen him go.

On they went until they were face to face with each other. the peliesman lept from his horse only to be stabed to the hart by Rupert then Tom jumped down and got Rupert a smart blow on the cheak.

Chapter VI

A DEADLY FIGHT

This enraged Rupert that that he shouted and made a plung but Tom was too quick for him artfully dogeing the sword he brout his sword round on Rupert's other cheak.

Just at that moment Ruper slashed killed the peliesmans horse then lept on Toms horse and golapt off.

Chapter VII

THE MYSTERIOUS MAN

Of cause ther was no chance of catching him on foot so Tom walked to the nearest inn to stay the night but it was ful up he had to share with another man.

Thou Tom was yery tired he could not sleep, their was something about the man he was he did not like he reminded him of some one he didnot know who.

Sudnly he felt something moveing on the bed looking up he saw the man fully dressed just gettimg off the bed

Chapter VIII

RUN TO ERTH

Now Ton could see that the mysteraous man was Rupert. Has he come to do a merder? Or has he only cometostay the night? thees were the thoughts that rushed throu Toms head.

he lay still to what Rupert would do first he opend a

cuberd and took out a small letter bag from this he too some
thing wich made Toms blud turn cold it was a bistol Tom
lept forward and seesed Rupert by the throught and flung
him to the ground

then snaching a bit of robe from the ground he bound
Rupert hand and foot.

Chapter IX

HUNG

then Tom drest hinself then Ton took Rupert to the
puliese cort Rupert was hung for killing the pulies man. I
hope the story will be a leson to you never to bet.

Shameful Reminiscence

IT IS UNFORTUNATE THAT THE MORE MEMORABLE OF ONE'S childish impressions should also be the more unprintable. Searching about in the cobwebbed corners of recollection—corners whose angles I had hitherto scarcely suspected—I find only spiders whose antics might possibly entertain Dr. Freud or Mr. Havelock Ellis, but whose resuscitation would scarcely appeal to that vague British bogey known generically as "The Censor." Who the Censor may be in actual fact I know not. Perhaps he does not even legally exist, outside his special domain of the theatre. But the great British public exists, and is entitled to write anonymous letters of protest to Scotland Yard; letters upon whose information Scotland Yard is liable to take action, scuttling the spiders back to their own obscure and dusty corners. Therefore the would-be sincere recorder of our difficult youthful years refrains from the interesting but manifestly scandalous recital, and takes refuge in the more innocuous but less poignant reminiscence of some social solecism; some dropped brick, which bruised the soul in its fall, quite unnecessarily, but for ever.

Thus, I may not record the morning when I gaily opened the unbolted bathroom door and discovered my naked godfather about to step into his bath; nor the morning when a small relative, aged five, took refuge behind the huge Chinese screen in the dining-room, and, overcome by shame and necessity, left a veritable puppy-puddle on the carpet. I may record only the tiny but indelible imprint of the occasion when I found Mrs. Thistlewaite alone in her own drawing-room.

The Thistlewaite children were my friends. There were five of them, four girls and a boy. The boy and I were allies; the four girls were our victims. The boy and I made a practice of tying the four girls up to trees and of thrashing their legs with nettles. Also, we stuffed their nostrils with putty, and gagged their mouths with handkerchiefs. No real hostility was implied in these activities. The girls enjoyed it masochistically, as much as the boy and I, sadistically, enjoyed it. It was during the period of the Boer War; the boy and I, respectively, were aged nine and eight; we wore khaki uniforms; he was Lord Roberts and I was Sir Redvers Buller; we had continual quarrels as to which should be Commander-in-Chief. We dug trenches in the garden, among the rhododendrons. We disagreed over almost every point: tactics, superiority of command, uniform, saluting. On one point only we were agreed: that we must bully the girls (i.e. the Boers) to the utmost extent possible.

We bullied them. They had a wretched time. I think they rather liked it.

Still, I preserved a feeling that however much the boy and I might maltreat the girls in private, I must personally maintain a certain standard of courtesy towards their mother.

Their mother was, indeed, a singularly charming woman. Child though I was, I recognised her delightful and mellow quality. Whenever I came into her presence, I realised that I should not have stuffed her daughters' nostrils with putty, or beaten their legs with nettles, even with the connivance and assistance of her son. She did not know about it, because her daughters were not the kind of daughters who sneak. Besides, their brother was involved. They might conceivably have betrayed *me*, but they would not have betrayed their brother.

Anyhow, I went one day to tea with my friends the Thistlewaites, my pocket stuffed with putty ready for fresh aggression.

For some reason, I was shown not into the schoolroom, but into the drawing-room where Mrs. Thistlewaite sat alone, stitching at her embroidery, under the pastel of her three elder daughters gazing into a blackbird's nest with three speckled eggs in it. It was a sentimental portrait, propped on an easel draped in a Paisley shawl; the drawing-room was so full of objects, little tables, consoles, chairs, and ornaments, that one could scarcely move without upsetting something. It was dominated by the triple portrait on the easel, and by Mrs. Thistlewaite, charming, placid, motherly, stitching at her embroidery. This, then, was the household into which I had introduced my putty and my nettles. . . .

Mrs. Thistlewaite made a movement as I came in.

"Oh, please!" I exclaimed, "don't get up."

I realised then that she had had no intention of getting up. She had merely reached forward for another skein of silk. Yet I had assumed that my introduction into that calm though over-crowded drawing-room would be a signal for her to get up. I was eight years old; she was, probably, forty. I was overcome by the shame of my involuntary patronage. "Please, don't get up," I had said; repeating only what I had heard grown-up people say; I had meant well, but then I put my hand furtively into my pocket, and found therein the lump of putty with which I had proposed to stuff her children's nostrils.

I looked again at the pastel of her daughters, gazing into the blackbird's nest. I felt very small indeed. I had besought Mrs. Thistlewaite not to get up. It was perhaps the first, and I hope the worst, but I dare not hope the last, social solecism that I ever committed.

The Tragic Years

IT IS FATALLY EASY TO BE SENTIMENTAL, OVER REMINIS-
cences of childhood. One is so apt to see oneself as a wistful,
pathetic, misunderstood little creature. And, indeed, to a
certain extent, all children *are* wistful, pathetic, misunderstood little creatures. But they are also hard-hearted,
egotistical, and uncivilised little creatures, and this aspect
of childhood is all too seldom touched upon, even in fiction.
In autobiography it is ignored altogether.

I propose, in fact, to ignore it myself.

No one who remembers me as a little girl has ever yet
told me that I was a nice child. Occasionally, it has been said
that I was an intelligent one, or a pretty one, or a precocious
one. Far more often I have been assured that I was a spoilt
child, a very tiresome child, and an exceedingly naughty
child.

As a matter of fact, the consciousness of being a naughty
child was early and thoroughly driven into me, and my
consequent cast-iron conviction that I must eventually go to
hell and burn there for ever and ever, would have done credit

to any member of the Fairchild family. It overshadowed the whole of life for me, from the time I was seven years old until long after I was, at least in the physical sense, "grown up."

Any reminiscences of my childhood, therefore, would make singularly gloomy reading—and the more honest they were, the gloomier they would be.

So that I propose to write freely of only one aspect of those days: that connected with the impulse that eventually led to my becoming a writer.

No one, so far as I know, has ever done me the dis-service of preserving any of my early efforts in the field of literature; but I have fairly vivid recollections of one or two unfinished masterpieces—usually in verse, and invariably tragic.

In those days, I liked an unhappy ending. I liked people to die, or to part from one another for ever, and I saw to it that in any composition of mine they did either one or the other, and very often both.

Indeed what strikes me most forcibly about my first attempts at writing, is the entire lack of humour that they evince, and the total absence of any feeling for reality. I had nearly added lack of originality as well; but perhaps that is not quite fair, for although my point of view was purely imitative, I do remember occasional startling individualities of expression.

For instance, I solved the difficulty of finding a line to rhyme with my dying soldier's farewell to his love: "Good-bye for evermore, my darling"—as follows:

"I'm flying upward like a starling,"

and this strange metaphor seemed to me not only ingenious, but highly poetical as well.

At seven or eight years old I began my first novel, which was to be called *Sylvia's Lost Brother*, and opened with the disappearance, in a thick London fog, of the infant Edward —brother of the heroine. I wrote four chapters—I think they must have been very short ones—and the *dénoument* to come was clear in my mind.

Sylvia, years later, orphaned, and—I need hardly say—bereft of her lover, was to be living alone in London, when one night a burglar was to enter the house, to be subsequently revealed as the lost Edward, and to die at her feet.

It is melancholy to have to add that the black manuscript book containing the germ of this remarkable effort was thrown into the water-butt by a younger sister—the only wilful injury, I think, that she ever did me in her life—and never retrieved.

At eleven, in the intervals of writing quantities of sentimental and very, very tragic verse, I covered a great deal of paper with the story of the Hamiltons. That manuscript survived for some years, and I re-read it at a later and more critical age.

There were six Hamiltons, young and beautiful, and they had an unkind stepmother, and sooner or later they all died, excepting one called Marjory, who went to the bad in some unspecified way and lived in London; but I feel sure that if I had ever finished the book she would have died too.

The Hamiltons, like King Charles, were an unconscionable time a-dying, and in the case of Aileen, aged 12, the sentence "Her blue eyes opened for the last time" occurred sixteen times in five pages.

After I went to school I stopped writing, except for a very occasional poem, until my sister and I started a private magazine. My contributions to it were numerous, and mostly very bad—all either pompous or sentimental. It was not until years later that it even occurred to me that one might possibly try, at least occasionally, to be amusing.

I was about fourteen when the story that was to be written and published long afterwards as *Zella Sees Herself*, first came into my mind. The character of Zella, the study of a very youthful *poseuse*, took shape almost exactly as I afterwards described her, but I meant the book to end—very characteristically—with Zella's suicide! When I eventually wrote it, however, I was in my twenties, and had at last outgrown my passion for tragedy.

The germ of *The Pelicans*—my third novel—also dates from my schoolroom days. I used to tell myself the story of the three girls, Rosamund, Frances and Hazel, and of the boy, Morris, while I practised the piano. Neither the central characters, nor the story itself, underwent much alteration when I came to write the book, more than ten years later.

Like all imaginative children, I lived largely in a world peopled by characters of my own invention. Almost all of them, I think, eventually found their way into one or other of my books. The excessive virtue and beauty of the women, and the tendency towards unbridled heroism and self-sacrifice of the men, had to be brought into line with the prosaic laws that govern life as it really is; but their fundamental characteristics, on the whole, remained unaltered.

What did alter, fortunately for me, was the profound and humourless gloom of my own outlook on life. But long before that amendment had taken place, the difficult, bewildering, often despairing, days of childhood, were over.

First Disobedience and the Fruit

"A REGULAR LITTLE HANDFUL," MY NURSE CALLED ME, for I was a reckless child, always tormenting my elder brother, and climbing over dangerous roofs, and pulling the wings off defenceless flies, and riding my father's favourite hunter. . . . Or would it be better to begin with the story of the strange old gentleman with reddish hair, who used to stop my perambulator on Wimbledon Common? And then I could go on to describe sitting on a lady's knee, while she read me a story her father had written called *The Rose and the Ring*, and Sir Frederick Poynter giving me my first box of water-colours, and how I hid under the piano to hear Ysaye play, and rebuked Archbishop Benson when he came to luncheon. . . . Or perhaps I had better admit that I was an odiously virtuous child, never greedy or sulky, always truthful, tidy and obedient, regarding my sisters with unkindly condescension, and always rushing to report their misdeeds. Then I could describe the enormous Palladian mansion, where I was brought up, and my voyages of exploration through suite after suite of gilded and tapestried saloons; or, still more romantic, the Haggerston tenement, where I lived with a drunkard father and helped to support an invalid mother by selling newspapers. . . .

All promising beginnings, and I do not know which I prefer. But, alas! they are daydreams; no Archbishop ever came to luncheon; I never saw Lady Ritchie; my father neither hunted nor tippled; and I had no brothers or sisters. But I did have two great-aunts, called Augusta and Georgina, who lived in a little house in Exeter, and one day, when they had some of the family to tea, Aunt Georgina was accused by her sister of taking her knitting-needles or some such crime—they were unmarried and inclined to quarrel— whereupon she exclaimed indignantly: "God knows, Augusta knows, it isn't true!" If then I make myself out other than a quite ordinary child living in a quite ordinary house, I risk being classed with Aunt Augusta, for I was distinguished only by a passionate love of reading, and an equally passionate hatred of all games in which a ball figured, except croquet. The name of the first person to play an important part in my life was not Swinburne but Reynolds (he was the gardener); and, though I learnt to read when I was four and began Latin when I was seven, I cannot pretend that in those days this was unusual. Indeed, I have searched my memory for any incident showing singularity or early force of character, but the best I can find is my obstinate refusal to learn to ride; and this I suspect was mere cowardice. I even dreaded being left alone in the governess-cart. All I can honestly boast of is that when I was eight, I used to play *petits chevaux* in the casinos of Northern France, and that I am one of the few living persons who have driven in a sledge behind a tandem over the snow-covered roads of Surrey.

Full of envy for my friends, who were all such unusual children, I fall back on a fortunate but commonplace incident which must have occurred when I was about six. I had been playing in a friend's garden, and when my nurse came for me, I refused to leave until I had said good-bye to a fox terrier to which I was attached. She insisted that I must go with her immediately, but I took no notice, and ran off to see the dog, which promptly bit my leg. (I have detested dogs ever since, noisy, coprophagous, limelight-loving animals, which always interrupt the conversation.) All my nurse said was that it was my own fault for being disobedient. She was Swiss and I was very fond of her, but I knew there was no possible relation of cause and effect between my naughtiness and the dog's bad temper. For the first time I realised that when it suited them, grown-ups were intellectually dishonest, and that if it came to moralising, no argument was too bad to be useful. From that moment I became a nonconformist with a small "n," driven by an irresistible impulse to the side of the minority. So it is not, I fear, reason and fastidiousness that have made me a Free Trader, for instance; it is a fox terrier. The result was considerable unhappiness at school and during the war, but enjoyment ever since—it is on the whole more interesting not to be on the side of the big battalions. Didn't I say that the incident was fortunate as well as commonplace?

"Mysterium Tremendum Fascinaus"

I REMEMBER WINDSOR FIRST OF ALL. MY FATHER WAS IN the Life Guards, and we lived at the Gables, Osborne Road. I can remember seeing Eton boys walking along the street, and a train coming into Windsor station, and how I thought that the funnel of the engine looked like an Eton boy's hat. But we soon left Windsor for Ireland, and crossed the sea from Milford to Waterford, when I found the bunks in which we slept interesting, but rather alarming. I as yet knew nothing about coffins, and did not come across these till later in Punch and Judy shows, when I found the death scenes very attractive, so there cannot have been that connection in my mind—a connection which Edgar Allen Poe described with noble skill—but still, there seemed to be something a little sinister about the whole business.

This journey was the beginning of sea journeys in my life, and it started something which has, I believe, influenced me ever since, in a way not always easy to analyse. Not long ago I talked about the sea with an Irish friend, and we both came to the conclusion that channel crossings had played a part in our lives which Englishmen might find hard to understand.

I was quite often brought over to England, and each time the journey gave me a definite sense of adventure, excitement, and romance. I feel it still. One night I can specially remember. It was a fine night, and to my five-year-old eyes, the mail steamer, all lighted up and belching smoke, seemed to stand for everything that is mysterious and attractive, as it came into sight on our way from the town station to the pier. Kingstown (now Dun Laoghaire; a pleasant name), Howth, North Wall, Greenore, Holyhead Race, South Stack; all these names still have a special significance for me; they stand for places which we passed at night, to the noise of fog-horns, the drumming of engines, and the splashing of waves. As a child, they seemed to belong to another world, like the places in the Tanglewood Tales, a book which frightened and delighted me. Perhaps Europa might have passed them when riding on her bull. Chester, Crewe, and Rugby also belonged to this weird world; but not being on the sea seemed of less importance. Still, they were wonderful places, great black domed stations, full of trains that roared and hissed in the night. The long journey that grown-up people found a little wearisome, gave me a sense of the mystery of this world, a sense which no materialist philosophy would ever satisfy. Since those days I have been on many night journeys on which I have known boredom and annoyance; but still, the sense has remained, as strong as ever. Only one thing do I find more mysterious, and that is the journey on a greater vessel, sometimes known as the Fisherman's Barque, on which it is my privilege to travel every day.

Fear played a large part in my life as a child, and I believe it does in the lives of most children, but being shamefully ignorant of psychology, I do not know the real reason why. My life was completely happy, with kindness on every side, but a strange dread of an unknown enemy was there all the same; not quite from the beginning, but very nearly so. There were places in our garden, in the thick woods that surrounded it, and in the winding passages of our house that seemed to me very sinister. I can also remember nightmares comical enough now, but at the time full of terror—horrible hands wearing grey gloves that had no body to control them, but ran about on their fingers with the motion of a centipede, and chased me with much hatred. I also had a great dread of the electric eel and the torpedo fish, animals described in my natural history book, and there were other more concrete enemies, such as the stewardesses on the mail steamer, who I believed were ready to kidnap children, and old Bess Kearon, a poor mad woman in the little seaport near our house. She had red eyes, and a grand descriptive Irish tongue, and used to pick quarrels with everyone in the street, hitting the boys with an old stick, spitting at her enemies, who were of her own choosing. Now and then she would yell a great stream of abuse which at the time I did not understand. Some of her words, which I thought must be foreign, sounded very fine; but I was told they were "rude," and not for me to use. To me she was always friendly, however, and would come and peer into the old-fashioned pony-carriage in which we drove about, leering and murmuring compliments in the Elizabethan language that one still hears in Ireland. This alarmed me a good deal.

When I was six years old I came up against real, concrete fear, and was genuinely frightened for the first time in my life. My body got slightly out of order, and an operation became necessary. When I was told this I was delighted. A relation of mine had had an operation the year before, and had been a highly important person for some time afterwards, talked about every day, so this must be a sign that I was growing up, and reaching the fame that I so justly deserved. It would also be a new adventure, like climbing trees or seeing the man hanged at Madame Tussaud's. I left for a Dublin nursing-home very much pleased with myself. But the reality. . . . A horrible mask held closely over my face, a disgusting smell, and all the terror of suffocation. Fear and rage fought for the first place in my mind, and I yelled the words I had heard Bess Kearon use.

Since then I have met many people who have been in hospitals and nursing-homes, and in most cases they have been satisfied—the poor are indeed full of praise for the London hospitals—but one thing I have met with time after time, children have been frightened by the anæsthetic. I feel this should not be. I have talked the matter over with several doctors, and it seems that if the child is frightened, it is almost always due to the clumsiness, or callousness, of the anæsthetist. It is possible to give an anæsthetic without causing distress. In my own case another operation was necessary a few months later, and instructions were given that the former performance was not to be repeated. A kinder doctor was employed, who knew his business, and all went off happily, but I shall not forget the horror of my first experience.

This was, however, the one dark spot in happy years. There were troubles, as when my governess found out that I told lies, mainly, I think, because it was such fun thinking them out, or when my tortoise died, and my aunt, to comfort me, made her meer-cat, an excellent animal rather like a mongoose, wear a black ribbon round its neck at the funeral; but the time slipped by, happy and contented: the journeys backwards and forwards to England, the great visit to the Dublin pantomime, and the discovery of books starting with the little stories in *Reading without Tears*, going right through the natural history book, and the *Cuckoo Clock*—the most genuinely imaginative book that has ever been written for children—and ending with delight at the ways of Sarah Gamp, some of whose references to Mrs. Harris, and her husband's behaviour on a certain occasion, I could not fully understand. At last I found myself, proudly dressed in a tweed suit and a huge bowler hat, crossing the sea once more, to go to a private school. I was no longer a child.

Going to Heaven

IF THE SUN IS SHINING, THE FIRST THING THAT I LOOK AT is always the sky.

If the sun is obscured, I can seldom see anything, except when the air assumes a light of its own, before storms. It is then twice as truthful, like a boy telling a lie.

All the illustrations in the books of my childhood shared the same background. Something like the Castle of Neuschwanstein, dominating a luxurious, impossible Greece. It was in these pictures that I discovered the sky. Blue of blues, white of whites, always the same, and always as it is still, the chief of all visible things that I find amiable and inspiring. *C'est le repos éclairè, ni fiévre, ni langueur....*

The sky remained in my books, as I remember it, until I was thirteen years of age. I was staying with my parents at Bad Kreuznach, and, one silent afternoon, my mother took me for a drive. The silence reminded me of recent summer days in a large London house, except that here I felt quite free, at last, of all mysterious terrors, such as that moment when one is standing in the hushed hall, believing everyone to be out, and a person looks down at one, too quickly, from the top of the stairs. We had an old, slow carriage, powdered with summer like a black plum, and all the journey was upwards, through land as still as if it had been in a greenhouse. Gliding up from the water-cold valleys, past vineyards, escarpments of coloured soils, we entered a warmer country of shadowless castles and towers, amazing in brilliance. As we passed, with infinite calm, the last castle, I noticed how the air suddenly began to hum and flash with evening. Topaz, Butter, Rose. New illuminations began to appear in various parts of the landscape, too sweet to describe.

We mounted, very slowly, the little hill behind the last castle, and drove into the sky. It was my first visit.

Early Snobberies

WHEN GROWN-UP PEOPLE WRITE OF CHILDHOOD, THEY write in the light of experience, which discolours the picture. Either they stress the continuity of their development, and say: "I am the same still"; or they stress the change, and say: "What an unpleasant child I was," which means: "How I have improved." I am inclined to the latter method.

I might say that, because I was born in the West of England, the beauties of that countryside could not but have left a deep impression on me; that I was in love with a vanishing agricultural England and with the English peasantry; that I took a premature interest in folk-dancing; that because there is a Celtic substratum in Somerset, I was prepared to understand a Celtic and agricultural country where I now live. But that would be quite untrue. I know that I took the beauties of nature for granted, and longed for towns; I found the village more interesting than the Mendip Hills; and when I went to the seaside resorts of the Bristol Channel, I preferred the High Street to the sands.

The main interests of country life were politics and

religion, and in both I was orthodox. I was an intellectual snob. I was a strong Conservative, and an Anglican, Broad to High. I handed plates of cakes to the Ladies' Committee of the local Unionist Association, and was given a small blue badge, a star with less points than usual, which must have been bogus, but increased my enthusiasm. During the elections of 1906 and 1910 I carried toy animals tied with blue bows; and I was always ready to subscribe, or to promise that my mother would subscribe to any organisation of a political, charitable or religious nature. Once I made a bad mistake, and enrolled myself in a Children's League, which was in fact Nonconformist. Before anyone knew, I had pledged myself, and sent in my name to a magazine of which I had read a single copy in the train. I lapsed, of course, as I did not consider Nonconformists and Liberals to be human; but for months I was afraid that the monsters would claim me.

The activities of the Church I found enthralling; and I shall never forget the day when the new Vicar increased the number of candles on the altar from two to six. I remember Wednesday as being my favourite day, because on Wednesday evenings in Lent and Advent there were services with special preachers. And I was proud of knowing much of the Prayer Book by heart, including the Athanasian Creed, which meant nothing to me, but was delightful because it was associated with feast-days. When I went to school and was taken to church on Ascension Day with the other girls, I was seen to have no prayer book during the creed. A mistress tapped me on the shoulder, and offered me one open at the words: "Neither confounding the persons, nor dividing the substance." I shouted them in her face, and at the same time pretended not to know what she was doing.

The earliest episode in my life that I can remember is connected with a theological student. He arrived on a bicycle from the neighbouring cathedral town, and was late for a picnic at which my mother wore a white dress, with a tight waist-band and an Indian filigree buckle, and bunches of cherries over her ears. I am told I could not have been more than three years old at the time; but he represented to me the perfection of beauty, intelligence and refinement. The special preachers seemed to me to have the same scholarly charm. And when at the age of nine, I went to school in the cathedral town, I found that all the girls were in love with theological students. We never met them, but admired from a distance the careless elegance of their belted tweed jackets on week-days, and on Sundays their hoods trimmed with rabbit-skin. Once when we were learning a geography lesson about Germany, we read that there were two thousand five hundred students at Göttingen, and one of the girls whispered: "How marvellous!"

I looked forward to being grown-up, used to do up my hair in secret and longed to wear high collars and tight waists. I thought it would be heaven to be at least as old as the top girls in the school; and at that time, from 1910 to 1914, girls of fifteen and sixteen seemed much older than they do now. I have photographs of groups of them with long skirts, masculine collars and ties, elaborate head-dresses of combs and ribbon, and earnest faces. A passage in literature which impressed me was in *The Wide, Wide World*, where the heroine, a schoolgirl, followed a difficult conversation in French among grown-ups, and when one of them forgot the name of an obscure battle, supplied it modestly and unobtrusively. I longed for that kind of triumph.

I was an ardent patriot and believed in German spies, though I admired the Kaiser, whom I saw riding a white horse at King Edward's funeral. I decided that the Kaiser himself knew nothing of the methods to which his under-lings had stooped. I liked the King of Spain best, however, of the visiting monarchs; and after him the King of Portugal. I was disappointed not to see the Czar, and when

I asked why he was not there, someone told me he "had other fish to fry"; so I did not enquire further.

During the war, we went to live in Oxford, and there I could indulge my admiration of clever young men. As the tougher ones were in the army, the atmosphere was especially refined and exotic. My first impression of undergraduates was that they were even more attractive than theological students, and that a lot of them were Indians. I had a passionate admiration for Oxford poets, and some were friends of my mother. Though I hardly dared speak to them, I studied their works, published by Mr. Blackwell in bright paper covers, and tried to imitate them in my school magazine. One kind of poem was mediævalist, with a title in Latin, and rhymed; another was Imagist, with a title in French, and did not. I remember writing a long mystical and allegorical poem called *The Alchemist*, a shorter one of modernist tendency about a train, and some prose poems reminiscent of the 'nineties. I also made complete collections of several short-lived reviews, and tried hard to make the school magazine more like them.

My favourite literary celebrity was really an Indian Moslem, who wrote nothing at all, at least in English, but said he could write poems in Persian. He used to read Swinburne aloud in a low monotonous voice and an exquisite foreign accent. I remember he was wearing a mauve shirt, a purple tie and a grey flannel suit one evening of a Summer Term, when he read *The Triumph of Time*; and I cried when he came to the line: "The rain has ruined the ungrown corn." I have never felt so mature since.

A
Seventeenth Century
Survival

THE CONSTITUENTS:—A WOMAN BORN IN 1820 IN ENNIS, County Clare, Ireland, brought up in a medieval economy (where even the candles were still home-made dips) of a fundamentalism so profound that even Tenessee to one of her depth would have seemed flighty. A man born in 1856 of a father who knew German theology yes, even Tubingen's, yet the son was converted and ordained "Low." Still the man and the woman could hardly apprehend each other, especially as the woman had to fill the position of resident mother-in-law, owing to her daughter's death. And three boys. The atmosphere:—Gloom. The mother having died when the youngest was three meant that the threshold of awareness was hung with crêpe. The first question ever remembered was whether new clothes must be bought, or whether everything worn might not be dyed black. There was no such focussed sense as the notion of a death, only that all life was naturally lightless as the world during an eclipse. And instruction confirmed this sense. "Remember, this is the happiest time of your life. When you grow up you will realise what a sad place the world is."

And there was every chance that you would not grow up. Had not the Matriarch buried nearly all her own large mid-Victorian brood? They had "declined" like interdependent ninepins, one after the other. Then, naturally, everything was incomparably blacker. For (a) it was certain that as yet you had not had the unmistakable convulsions that marked you as "converted," and (b), unconverted you were "lost." Ergo, we three whose expectation of life was meagre nevertheless only had that none too bright connection to save us from an incomparably worse disaster. Life was dreary: death was literally and fundamentally, hell. In vain one questioned: "Aren't I saved?" There could only be one answer. As certain as an unswollen arm demonstrates that the protective vaccine has not worked, so certainly the unconvulsed mind proved that it had not won its salvation. Still the faith was not without works. Night soon became a terror beside which every physical pain was better to be borne. Was not this a sign of having accepted the doctrine? "No," we were warned: "'The devils believe and tremble'; conviction is not enough."

Still it was something to work on, and a nurse, employed because she knew the pass-words of Evangelicalism, but who found, perhaps naturally, more comfort in alcoholic spirits, played on these night terrors. The high eighteenth century house must be mounted in the dark alone, and the bedroom found and the bed entered in the dark. Nor, with the noblest motives, was the Matriarch much behind in enforcing these disciplines. With terror of devils went nauseating horror at the grave's corruption. By an odd chance someone had given us a set of papier mâché and wire skeletons, but they awoke such terrific disgust in me that, in a freak of mercy, they were hidden; until one day this irrational concession was questioned by a brother, the Matriarch sustained the appeal, and while she looked on, the squeamish one was held on the floor by the two elder brothers, and the obscene objects rubbed on his face. Then, indeed, a convulsion was experienced, but one that did not qualify for heaven; on the contrary, it was certified as an attack of such temper as to warrant real punishment.

In such a universe how defend oneself? At night one could only stick it out huddled as one's tree-top ancestors, till light came. In the day a hierarchy of physical forces, second brother, eldest brother, nurse, Matriarch, father, ringed one in, rising one behind the other, forbidding height beyond forbidding height. The defence of the weak is the lie. Beside, to the terror-stretched mind fantasy is all too easy. Therefore steps must be taken to crush this defence. "The child's will must be broken" often ruled the Matriarch. The lie, whether believed by the desperate defender or no, was ruled a capital offence. There was a service for the condemned. A passage from that fantasy, the Apocalypse, was read, because from that portion of Writ could be established that liars were allotted the worst place in hell. If that was their undoubted due, human power must attempt to prepare the way for divine justice, and the condemned one was handed over to the male, if not secular, arm. That was the principal manifestation of the paternal presence in the home. It was understood that bereavement had bowed that person so low that only could he bring himself to make contact with the reminders of his woe at the high call of justice and in order to render them at least as woeful as himself. Filial affection is evidently, according to modern authorities, always a tender growth and under this treatment it soon wilted.

A childish world of nightmare and petty violence. But an admirable introduction to a century as volcanic as this has proved. To those who stepped from the steadily deepening security of the normal nineteenth century home out into the storms of the twentieth century world, life has proved to be a much ruder thing than they were led to expect when they were young. But for those who stepped straight out of the seventeenth century into this, it has not proved anything like so disconcerting or unexpected. The romantics see behind them sunset splendours, but one who has actually been brought up near that eternal bonfire knows how deceptive are the picturesque colourings that at sufficient distance appear to drape it. And even dread of instant war and revolution, how pale such fires are beside the authentic fear of hell. Growing out of such a childhood has been coming like Proserpine up to the day. True, your weather up here may often be pretty poor, but here there are limits. There, there were none.

An archaic childhood for 1889 to 1899, when its worst horrors ceased, but perhaps accountable for an optimism still persisting in 1932.

Childhood

THE DIFFICULT THING IS TO REMEMBER IT.

I remember, in 1887, when the old Queen's first Jubilee
was being celebrated, being given a golden sovereign in a
stable-yard, by a tall stranger, whose name I never knew. I
remember the unveiling, by the Crimean-whiskered Lord
Mount Edgcumbe of that day, of the Armada Memorial, on
Plymouth Hoe, my sister and I hanging tightly to a nurse's
hands, and the place covered with troops and volunteers.
"Volunteers"—how antediluvian the word sounds! Yet our
bootmaker (or "snob" as the term then was), stout and side-
whiskered and patently unfit for service, distended his cheeks
to a bugle in the volunteers, wearing a Rifleman's green-
faced uniform, and a hat with a shaving-brush sticking up
from it.

I think I heard Mr. Gladstone speak from the balcony
of the Grand Hotel to a vast assemblage in the twilight, I
being lifted up. But did I? Or is memory playing tricks? I
must look it up. If he was there, I was.

But I know that when I was six or seven the shadow of

death came over me. She was a year or two older. I think her name was Hilda; but I cannot be sure. Her parents are now probably dead, and if she had brothers and sisters, they will remember her dimly, if at all, for it was forty years ago. We hadn't said very much. We had merely sat, occasionally, on benches looking down at the mighty placid Sound, with our nurses, and caught eyes and touched hands. And once or twice we had paddled together.

Then one day I heard she had gone to the Ladies' Bathing Place (which in itself is an echo from a departed epoch, like Caroline Place and Adelaide Place), and had been drowned. I could not realise it. In my bed at night I tried to call her back. Now I am uncertain of her name. But she had an eager, candid, freckled little face, and she went without any sort of fulfilment.

And the unconscious tides still ebbed and flowed; and the sun sparkled on the wavelets; and at low water I cut my feet on the sharp rocks, and peered into the fathomless pools at anemones, and scuttling crabs and minnows, and pebbles and shells, isolated for some hours from the deep, and slithered on dark rocks slimed over by cabbage-green weed, and only sometimes remembered the child who had been drowned.

OXFORD

MORE OXFORD PAPERBACKS

Details of a selection of other books follow. A complete list of Oxford Paperbacks, including The World's Classics, Twentieth-Century Classics, OPUS, Past Masters, Oxford Authors, Oxford Shakespeare, and Oxford Paperback Reference, is available in the UK from the General Publicity Department, Oxford University Press (JH), Walton Street, Oxford, OX2 6DP.

In the USA, complete lists are available from the Paperbacks Marketing Manager, Oxford University Press, 200 Madison Avenue, New York, NY 10016.

Oxford Paperbacks are available from all good bookshops. In case of difficulty, customers in the UK can order direct from Oxford University Press Bookshop, 116 High Street, Oxford, Freepost, OX1 4BR, enclosing full payment. Please add 10% of published price for postage and packing.

ON A CHINESE SCREEN
W. Somerset Maugham

Introduction by H. J. Lethbridge

This remarkable book resulted from Maugham's travels in China between 1919 and 1920 and was first published in 1922. It presents in a sequence of vignettes and brief sketches an extraordinary range of the European types then resident there: missionaries and their wives, Catholic priests and nuns, consular and diplomatic officials, taipans and business men, soldiers and seafarers, and all the flotsam and jetsam of European communities in the East. There are Chinese among the portraits as well, including an official who was supremely sensitive to beauty in all its forms and yet grossly venal in his public life and a Chinese professor of comparative literature who made wonderfully bizarre evaluations of foreign writers.

Since Maugham visited China the treaty ports have gone, the privileged expatriate communites have vanished, and the visitor is no longer free to wander at will. *On a Chinese Screen* is now an important historical document.

A GRAMMAR OF THE ENGLISH LANGUAGE
William Cobbett

Introduction by Robert Burchfield

William Cobbett's radicalism brought him into conflict with the authorities on many occasions, but he reserved a special kind of venom for politicians like Lord Castlereagh and the Duke of Wellington, and for men of letters such as Dr Johnson, Dr Isaac Watts, and Fellows of English Colleges whose writing, he declared, 'show their command of grammar is no better than that of chambermaids, hucksters, and plough-boys'. He takes them all to task for their lamentable standard of English in his *Grammar*, first published in 1818, and revised in 1823. It is the most colourful treatment of the subject ever published, both highly prejudiced and richly illustrated with examples drawn from the language of the countryside.

'trenchant, funny, one of the key texts in the field of language and politics, by one of the greatest of Englishmen' *Sunday Times*

STILL GLIDES THE STREAM

Flora Thompson

Like her well-loved trilogy *Lark Rise to Candleford,* this book depicts the vanished life of the countryside which Flora Thompson knew as a child in the 1880s. Cast in a fictional form, it is an enchanting portrait of an Oxfordshire village and its inhabitants around the time of Queen Victoria's Golden Jubilee.

'reading it is a perfect pleasure' *Benny Green*

THE AUTOBIOGRAPHY OF A SUPER-TRAMP

W. H. Davies

Preface by George Bernard Shaw

This is the classic account of the poet W. H. Davies's adventures as a young man travelling around America and England at the turn of the century. His spare, evocative prose gives raw power to his experiences among tricksters, down-and-outs, and itinerant labourers, and makes the characters he encounters—New Haven Baldy, the Indian Kid, and Boozy Bob—unforgettable.

'Anyone reading this book will turn back to Davies's poems with renewed respect. Their lyrical fineness had been forged in a hard school, the *Autobiography,* like *Amaryllis,* is the real thing.' Glen Cavaliero, *T.E.S.*

THE OLD SCHOOL

Edited by Graham Greene

An entertaining and often very funny collection of essays about the school-days of some of the best writers of our time.

Includes: Anthony Powell on Eton, W. H. Auden on Gresham's School, Holt, H. E. Bates on Kettering Grammar School, Elizabeth Bowen on Downe House, L. P. Hartley on Harrow, William Plomer on Rugby, Stephen Spender on University College School, Harold Nicolson on Wellington, Arthur Calder-Marshall on St Paul's, and many others.

'A classic collection.' *Sunday Times*

LATER DAYS

W. H. Davies

In this sequel to *The Autobiography of a Super-tramp,* Davies describes his early career as a writer, and his friendships with Hilaire Belloc, Edward Thomas, George Bernard Shaw, and other eminent literary figures of the period. He never lost his love of the open road, and he tells of his travels round England when, in his down-and-out years (and despite having only one leg), he went from village to village peddling lace, pins, and needles.

THE JOURNAL OF A SOMERSET RECTOR, 1803–1834

John Skinner

With an essay by Virginia Woolf

Edited by Howard and Peter Coombs

John Skinner's journal reveals many truths about life in rural England at the beginning of the nineteenth century. He spares us no detail of the appalling social conditions and injustices he found in his small country parish. Virginia Woolf's brilliant essay hints at a special affinity she felt with this neurotic, introspective man, who, as she herself was to do, fell victim to a final suicidal depression.

'An extraordinary document, historically and personally.' *Country Life*

'a great find . . . fascinating' *Open History*

'a fascinating insight into the poverty and suffering which was English rural life during and after the Napoleonic wars' *Tribune*

JAMES JOYCE

Richard Ellmann

Winner of the James Tait Black and the Duff Cooper Memorial Prizes

Professor Ellmann has thoroughly revised and expanded his classic biography to incorporate the considerable amount of new information that has come to light in the twenty-two years since it was first published. The new material deals with most aspects of Joyce's life: his literary aims, a failed love affair, domestic problems, and his political views.

'The greatest literary biography of the century.' Anthony Burgess

'Richard Ellmann's superb biography . . . [is] a great feat of twentieth-century literary scholarship.' Christopher Ricks

'A superlatively good biography of Joyce.' Frank Kermode, *Spectator*

THE GATES OF MEMORY

Geoffrey Keynes

Geoffrey Keynes had, as he put it himself, 'a quite outrageously enjoyable existence'. This is his remarkable account of a long and distinguished life, written only two years before his death in 1982.

The younger brother of the economist Maynard Keynes, Geoffrey Keynes was at Rugby and Cambridge with Rupert Brooke. He saved Virginia Woolf from her first suicide attempt, became a celebrated surgeon who pioneered the use of blood transfusion and the rational treatment of breast cancer, and was knighted for this work in 1955.

'less an autobiography than a valuable piece of social history . . . a portrait of an age' Anthony Storr, *Sunday Times*

P. G. WODEHOUSE

A Literary Biography

Benny Green

'A fine study not superseded by Frances Donaldson's recent authorized biography. Green's analysis of Orwell and Wodehouse, for example, is revelatory.' *Sunday Times*

'An affectionate and witty biography reminding us how dull the world would be without the antics of Wodehouse's amiable lunatics.' *Sunday Telegraph*

THE RISE AND FALL OF A REGENCY DANDY

The Life and Times of Scrope Berdmore Davies

T. A. J. Burnett

Foreword by Bevis Hiller

The Literary Discovery of the Century was how *The Times* headlined the finding of a trunk more than 150 years old in a London bank vault in 1976. It had belonged to Scrope Berdmore Davies, dandy, wit, gambler, rake, and one of the legendary circle that surrounded the young Byron, and contained everything he might have needed to write his memoirs—notebooks of Byron and Shelley, letters, bills from fashionable gaming clubs, and much more. T. A. J. Burnett has used this unique material to reconstruct in vivid detail the life and times of a Regency dandy.

'a fascinating look at a Regency rascal.' *Sunday Times*

'Illuminating, absorbing and sharply detailed'. Christopher Hibbert

'Learned and fascinating.' Auberon Waugh

W. H. HUDSON

A Biography

Ruth Tomalin

A well-researched and detailed biography of the finest nature-writer of the Victorian age.

'Ruth Tomalin's book will probably become the standard life.' *New Statesman*

'Well-researched and well-written.' Wynford Vaughan-Thomas, *Nature*

'Pleasing and detailed.' Paul Theroux, *Sunday Times*

THE ORDEAL OF IVOR GURNEY

Michael Hurd

Behind the name of Ivor Gurney lies the tragic story of a composer and poet whose life seemed full of promise but who ended his days in a mental hospital.

In his biography of this exceptional man, Michael Hurd draws on a wealth of material, including Gurney's brilliant and amusing letters and the extraordinary poems that chronicle so movingly his descent into madness.

'Ivor Gurney . . . admirably portrayed here by the composer Michael Hurd, is of compelling and tragic interest'. Anthony Storr, *Sunday Times*

'After this biography, Ivor Gurney's name will never again flicker minimally in the anthologies and song repertoires, as it has for so many years.' Ronald Blythe, *Listener*

THE HEIRS OF TOM BROWN

The English School Story

Isabel Quigly

The Heirs of Tom Brown is an entertaining and original investigation into the literary, social, and cultural history of the school story in the heyday of the English Public School. Isabel Quigly discusses her chosen stories in relation to the themes which recur most frequently throughout the genre—the cult of games, the love story, the boarding school as a training ground for the Empire, schoolboy heroics, and an extraordinary preoccupation with death. Her selection ranges from such masterpieces as *Stalky & Co.* and Wodehouse's cricketing stories, to the schoolgirl tales of Angela Brazil, and the scandalously subversive *The Loom of Youth*.

'an excellent guide to this curious but interesting chapter in social and literary history' *Listener*

'It's hard to recall a more telling analysis.' *Sunday Times*

'clear-sighted and enjoyable' *Financial Times*

LETTERS TO VENETIA STANLEY

H. H. Asquith

This paperback edition of the letters of H. H. Asquith, Prime Minister, to the young Venetia Stanley who he adored, includes letters discovered in 1984. Almost all written between January 1912 and May 1915, the letters are loving, informative, and amusing. Whenever he could not meet her, Asquith wrote to Venetia; sometimes three times a day, sometimes during a debate in the House of Commons, sometimes even in a Cabinet meeting. Early in 1914 he began to write to her about politics, divulging military secrets and freely discussing such colleagues as Lloyd George, Churchill, and Kitchener.

Equally arresting is the personal story of Venetia Stanley who was also loved by and eventually married to Edwin Montague, a junior Cabinet Minister in his thirties. The letter in which she told Asquith of her engagement reached him at a time of crisis in his and his country's wartime fortunes.

FIRST CHILDHOOD AND FAR FROM THE MADDING WAR

Lord Berners

'Aesthete, artist, and wit, Lord Berners grew up amoung fox-hunting philistines and attended a prep-school where excellence at games, to which he did not aspire, provided the only refuge from a sadistic headmaster. *First Childhood* is a wry record of his early kicks against the pricks, while *Far From the Madding War* is a delightful novella set in wartime Oxford with a thinly disguised self-portrait which anticipates Nancy Mitford's Lord Merlin.' *Books and Bookmen*

'Lord Berners spices his very funny account of a rather isolated and unhappy childhood, *First Childhood,* with a wicked wit.' *British Books News*

'It is a bargain and a delight—particularly the autobiography . . . by any standards an absorbing book.' *Times Literary Supplement*

AN AUTOBIOGRAPHY
1: 1880–1911
Leonard Woolf

Leonard Woolf (1880–1969), disciple of reason, colonial civil servant, author, editor, journalist, politician, publisher, husband of Virginia, was one of the central figures of the Bloomsbury group, and indeed of the English intellectual life of his time. His widely acclaimed autobiography, originally published in five volumes, now appears, unabridged, in a two-volume Oxford Paperbacks edition. This first volume, incorporating *Sowing* and *Growing,* covers the author's childhood, his years at Cambridge, and his service as an increasingly reluctant 'imperialist administrator' in Ceylon, service which came to an end in 1911 with his decision to resign, partly in the hope of marrying Virginia Stephen.

For this new edition Quentin Bell, Virginia Woolf's nephew and biographer, has written an introduction which gives us a telling personal portrait of Leonard Woolf.

'Mr Woolf's memoirs are centrally, important documents of our cultural history in this century.' *Guardian*

'The great quality in Woolf as an autobiographer is his utter truthfulness—rarer in this genre of literature than one might suppose.' Malcolm Muggeridge

'The narrative of the years which culminated in Cambridge is extraordinarily well done . . . Mr Woolf writes in an incisive, vigorous prose, admirably suited to his own uncompromising view of life.' Anthony Powell

CARRINGTON

Letters and Extracts from her Diaries

Edited by David Garnett

Gifted painter, intimate companion of Lytton Strachey, friend of Virginia Woolf, Augustus John, Ottoline Morrell, and E. M. Forster, Dora Carrington led an extraordinary life. In her late teens she escaped from her respectable middle-class home to enter the bohemian world of the Slade School of Art and the artistic and intellectual circles centred on Bloomsbury and Garsington. At the age of twenty-two she met Lytton Strachey. He was a homosexual and an intellectual; she detested her own feminity and had been haphazardly educated. Nevertheless, they formed a deeply affectionate relationship which survived their sexual difficulties, separations, and infidelities until Strachey's death. Three months later, unable to contine life alone, Carrington shot herself.

Superbly edited by David Garnett, this book constitutes one of the most candid, entertaining, and moving autobiographies ever written.

'Handsome and splendidly edited.' Paul Levy, *Observer*